Famous Biographies for Young People

FAMOUS AMERICAN INDIANS

by William Heuman

ILLUSTRATED WITH PHOTOGRAPHS
AND OLD PRINTS

FAMOUS BIOGRAPHIES
DM
FOR YOUNG PEOPLE

Dodd, Mead & Company · New York

To Frank Fensterer

Printed in the United States of America
by Vail-Ballou Press, Inc., Binghamton, N. Y.

CONTENTS

Illustrations follow page 64

"Let me be a free man—free to travel, free to stop, free to work, free to trade where I choose, free to choose my own teachers, free to follow the religion of my fathers, free to think and talk and act for myself—and I will obey every law or submit to the penalty. Whenever the white man treats the Indian as they treat each other, then we will have no more wars. We shall all be alike—brothers of one father and one mother, with one sky above us and one country around us, and one government for all."—*Chief Joseph of the Nez Percé*

KING PHILIP

[1639–1676]

THE GROUP of stern-faced white men in their black, wide-brimmed hats, buckled shoes, and knee pants watched in silence as the file of Wampanoags came out of the woods, walking toward the Taunton, Massachusetts, meetinghouse this spring of 1671.

The tall Indian, Philip, known as King Philip to Indians and whites alike, walked at the head of the group, a mantle of turkey feathers and squirrel skins over his shoulders.

The white men whispered to each other, nodding toward the Indian chief, whose dark eyes were fixed straight ahead of him as he moved with a light, easy tread toward the meetinghouse.

This was the Wampanoag chieftain who, it was said, was secretly preparing for war against the whites throughout the colony of Massachusetts. Now he was being called to account by the white men who wanted to know why he was trying to obtain guns for his people, why he was visiting other New England tribes having secret consultations with them.

Fifty years before, on another spring day exactly like this, another tall Indian had walked, unannounced, into the single street of the new town of Plymouth in America. Plymouth was not very much of a town in the year 1621. Just a few months earlier, the townspeople, known as Pilgrims, religious refugees from England, had stepped ashore from a battered, leaky little ship known as the *Mayflower*.

Hastily, they'd raised their log cabins with the thatched roofs and the crude stone chimneys, and then they had nearly starved the remainder of the winter. Now in the spring food supplies were very low and the leaders of the settlement were wondering how they could possibly feed the people until summer and fall when the first crops came in.

The Pilgrims stared in surprise as the lone Indian strode through the village of Plymouth. Some of the men took their blunderbusses from the pegs on the walls. The women and children watched fearfully.

The tall Indian was smiling, though, holding up his right hand in a gesture of friendship. When several of the men finally approached him, he said, "Welcome, Englishmen."

The Pilgrims had been aware of the presence of Indians in the vicinity of Plymouth, and they'd kept a close guard throughout the winter, but they'd had no contact with them.

The arrival, therefore, of an Indian who spoke to them in English was indeed a surprise. They discovered that his name was Samoset, and that he'd learned to speak a little English from fishermen he'd met along the Maine coast.

Samoset was a chief of the Pemaquids and a friend of Massasoit, chief of the Wampanoags who lived in the vicinity of the colony. Soon after his meeting with the whites in Plymouth Town, Samoset brought Massasoit and a few of his braves in for a visit. The Pilgrims, realizing how few they were and how weak in this country, went to extremes in their greeting of the Wampanoag chief.

A trumpet blared and the drums beat as Massasoit was led to one of the cabins. A rug had been spread on the floor for him to sit on.

The colonists greeted Massasoit in the name of James the First of England, and then asked for an alliance with the Wampanoags.

The friendly Massasoit, a good and just man, agreed to the alliance, even putting a mark on a piece of paper which the white men stated was a treaty of peace.

Later in the spring the Wampanoags taught the colonists how to plant corn by putting a dead fish in each of the mounds as fertilizer. They taught them how to hunt for deer and turkey.

There were visits by the Pilgrims to the Wampanoag village of Pokanoket where the Indians greeted the colonists courteously. In the fall of 1621 the Pilgrims and the Wampanoags joined together to celebrate the first Thanksgiving in America, the Wampanoags providing the deer and the wild turkey.

Until he died in 1661, Massasoit was the true friend of the white man. As a matter of fact, he even sought English names—Alexander and Philip—for his two sons, Wamsutta and Metacomet.

It was this same Philip—King Philip, son of Massasoit— who walked down the dirt street of Taunton that spring day of 1671, fifty years later.

In fifty years tremendous changes had taken place. More and more English ships had come into Narragansett Bay, landing hundreds and hundreds of white men and women, establishing towns—Taunton, Deerfield, Salem, Marblehead, Boston.

The Wampanoags, and the other tribes in the vicinity, had been a happy people, living in their bark houses, planting corn and squash and melon, hunting for deer, turkey, and other game. Along the shores of the Bay they'd dug clams; they'd caught fish and scallops.

The whites were no longer confined to a single little village set back from the shore of the Bay. There were thousands upon thousands of them in the land, and they did not greet an Indian chief now as an equal.

They'd taken over much of the land, bartering for it with guns and blankets; they'd purchased land outright from chiefs who could never understand why the white man wanted so much land that he could never use. The Indians had no conception of land ownership. The land was like the sky, the water; it belonged to all.

The white man gave the Indian a gun for a large tract of land. The Indian was very happy to receive the gun, but he was quite surprised when the white man refused to let him plant corn on the land.

The white man, of course, saw it differently. Land was a commodity; land represented wealth and security. Upon it he built his house, his castle, and there he lived with his family, raising his crops, sustaining himself. It was his forever, so said English law.

Hence the anxiety when it was learned that King Philip of the Wampanoags was hoarding guns, holding secret consultations with neighboring tribes. The settlers demanded that he desist.

As a sign that Philip was not planning on war against the whites it was demanded that he give up his guns. Reluctantly, and with hatred in his heart, Philip turned over to the colonists the few guns his people possessed. He realized that his Wampanoags could never wage war successfully against the settlers on their own. What was needed was an alliance—an alliance of warriors from other tribes in Massachusetts and Rhode Island, fighting men from the Sakonnets, the Pocassets, the powerful Nipmucks, possibly even the Narragansetts, who'd always been the hereditary enemies of the Wampanoags.

Already, Philip, a clever diplomat, wise to the ways of the white man who'd been taking land from his people for a generation by fair means or foul, had been in contact with the other tribes, seeking to form an alliance with them.

"When the English first came here," Philip said to the other chieftains, "they were few and hungry. My father fed them and helped them. Then more and more of them arrived, and they took from us tract after tract so that we now have little land left. But I shall not live to be without country."

Even in his father's day, as more settlers had come, there had been difficulties with the colonists, white men trying to buy land with firewater and trinkets, duping Indians into selling enormous tracts of their hunting grounds, unable to make them understand that they could no longer hunt or plant on these lands.

Massasoit had maintained the peace, placating his tribesmen. Philip realized by now that peace was impossible with a people who were constantly pushing at them, gobbling up the land. Soon there would be none left.

Before the Taunton meeting, therefore, he'd traveled through the New England forests, forming friendships with distant tribes. The English had watched him constantly, knowing that he was up to something but unable to pin him down.

Skillfully, Philip bided his time. He made concessions to the colonists; he gave up guns to maintain the peace but always with the thought that some day he and his allies would be strong enough to drive the whites back into the sea from which they'd come.

Four years after the meeting in Taunton, hostilities broke out. In June of 1675 a Wampanoag who had been educated by missionaries revealed to the English that Philip was actively plotting war against them, a war which was soon to break out.

In retaliation for this betrayal the informer was killed. Three Wampanoags were arrested, tried, and condemned to death for the murder.

After the hanging of the Wampanoags, Philip was enraged. The whites had no authority over his people. Even the English king had recognized Philip as the ruler of the Wampanoags. The murderers should have been turned over to him.

Near the village of Pokanoket was the small English settlement of Swansea. A party of Wampanoags went to the village and shot down some cattle.

The townspeople of Swansea rushed to the garrison house and the Wampanoags plundered the village. One of the braves was shot and King Philip's War was on, even though Philip knew that he was not yet ready for the conflict. Fervently, he hoped that the other tribes would now join with him in his fight against the English.

Immediately he sent messages to the tribes, and then he sent the Wampanoag women and children to the land of the Narragansetts. Because the village of Pokanoket was located on a peninsula it was imperative that the Wampanoags get back to the mainland before the English cut them off.

The colonists grasped this fact, also, and sent a fleet of small boats to ring the peninsula. At the same time a large party of armed men headed for Pokanoket.

Philip and his people managed to make their escape, moving into a swamp area on the mainland. The English tram-

pled down their cornfields and burned the houses of Pokanoket.

From his swamp hideout, Philip and his Wampanoags
struck out in every direction, hitting at the towns of Rheo-
both, Taunton, and Middleborough. The fearful colonists
didn't know where Philip would strike next with his "red
devils." They moved into the garrison houses and stockaded
forts, leaving the countryside open.

Several hundred men marched toward Philip's hide-out,
and Philip cleverly enticed them deeper into the swamp, retreating with a small party of his warriors. By nightfall the
English force had lost many men. Dazed and beaten, they retreated from the swamp.

The colonists built an armed camp near the hide-out and
sent patrols into the swamp. The Wampanoags now built
rafts and floated across the Taunton River to escape.

The colonists next enlisted the aid of tribes which had always been enemies of the Wampanoags—the Mohicans and
others. The war was widening.

Philip by now was receiving aid, also. The Nipmucks to
the northwest had joined in the fighting against the whites.
In the small town of Boston the colonial leaders tried to negotiate with the Nipmucks, sending a peace delegation, but
most of the delegates were ambushed and killed by the Nipmucks, who then hit at the frontier settlement of Brookfield.
The cabins around Brookfield were plundered and the settlers besieged in their blockhouse. A party of dragoons eventually rescued them.

Philip and his Wampanoags now joined the Nipmucks
and hit at the colonists up and down the Connecticut River
Valley. Deerfield and Northfield were hastily abandoned.
The town of Springfield was burned. Settlers were killed and

scalped throughout New England.

At a small stream, known today as Bloody Brook, a 100-man expedition which had been hauling wagonloads of corn to the town of Hadley was ambushed by a large war party and only a few white men escaped.

It was a bitter war. There were atrocities on both sides. Indians and white men scalped each other indiscriminately, and when parties of Indian prisoners were brought in, men, women and children were oftentimes sold to slavers and shipped to the West Indies.

Armed white forces overran Indian villages, destroying them completely, burning the corn crops and the houses with their caches of food.

The red allies were equally vindictive. Prisoners were taken only infrequently. Men, women, and children were struck down in the raids. There was no pity. Indian raiding parties came with the first light of dawn. The war whoops resounded through village streets, around isolated farmhouses.

Through the months of September, October, and November of 1675 the fighting continued, but by now the Indians were becoming tired of it. To an Indian, war had always been a matter of a quick raid, a sudden onslaught, victory or defeat, and then it was over. The white man, they discovered, did not fight this way. He kept coming, forever, and the continued struggle did not appeal to the Indians.

With winter approaching, and most of the corn crop destroyed, the Indian allies had to think about food. It was necessary to hunt for meat for the winter.

As far as the Wampanoags and their allies were concerned, they had defeated the English, wiping out many of their settlements, and it was foolish to go on fighting.

Philip knew, though, that this line of reasoning was false.

14

The English were still there. They would come back stronger than ever. The only way was to get rid of them now —*all of them.*

He sought help from the fierce Mohawks to the south, trying to convince this strong tribe that his fight was their fight, too, but the Mohawks had been engaged in a profitable fur trade with the English, and, besides, they had no quarrel with the whites who had not yet started taking over *their* lands.

Philip turned to the Narragansetts, once his bitter enemies. He was at first unsuccessful, but then the English literally drove the Narragansetts into his camp.

Some Pocassets, Philip's allies, had taken refuge with the Narragansetts, and now the English colonists of Massachusetts, Rhode Island, and Connecticut, realizing that they needed a single, unified force to hit at the Indians, formed an army of several thousand men. A thousand of these marched toward the Narragansett village and demanded that the Narragansett chief, Canonchet, hand over the Pocassets to them.

Canonchet, who was now in sympathy with Philip and beginning to realize that it was impossible to exist alongside the whites, refused to give up the refugees. His village was located on high ground in a swamp, a log stockade surrounding it.

Canonchet had three thousand people in the village with him, and the only way to reach the village was over a narrow, secret trail through the marshes.

At first the powerful white force was not too anxious to march through the terrible swampland and hit at the Narragansetts, but a renegade Indian offered to guide them over the trail.

It was a mid-December day, freezing cold, when the white

force moved down the narrow trail through the marshes toward Canonchet's village. Reaching the walls they charged again and again, finally making a breach in the stockade.

The Narragansetts and the Pocassets had only a few guns and their ammunition was soon used up. More than six hundred of the Indian men, women, and children were killed in the fight inside the stockade before Canonchet retreated.

The worn-out English forces had lost many men, also, and they were glad to get out of the swamp and back to their base camp. It had been the bloodiest fight of the war.

Canonchet and his Narragansetts now joined with Philip. Nipmucks, Narragansetts, and Philip's Wampanoags hit in every direction. Their warparties roamed throughout Massachusetts, Rhode Island, and Connecticut. More than a dozen settlements were burned. Hundreds of families were massacred.

Out of ninety settlements in New England at the outbreak of the war, at least half had been hit by the red allies. Philip's Wampanoags even struck at Plymouth and set houses on fire.

Philip's grip on the Indian allies was loosening now, though. Mohicans and Pequots, convinced that he could not win in this conflict with the whites, joined the enemy.

Canonchet was captured by a party of colonists, Mohicans, and Pequots and taken to Stonington. There he was offered his life if he would help the white men fight against Philip.

The loyal Canonchet said, "I shall die before my heart is soft or I have said anything unworthy of myself."

Not only was Canonchet put to death by the colonists, but his wife and children with him. The death of Canonchet was a severe blow to Philip.

With their Indian allies assisting them, the whites went

on the offense, hitting at Indian camps in the wilderness. One of Philip's staunchest allies, the Sakonnets, broke with him, joining the colonists.

With the help of the Sakonnets, the English found Philip's secret quarters and hit at him there. Over a hundred Wampanoag warriors were killed. Philip, himself, managed to escape, but his wife and son were captured and sold into slavery in the West Indies. The red alliance broke up like river ice in the spring thaw.

The Narragansetts, like the Sakonnets, had had enough of the war after the death of Canonchet. The Nipmucks, too, gave up the fight. Hoping for leniency, some Nipmucks even brought their war chief into Boston, turning him over to the authorities.

Hounded from place to place, and almost alone now, Philip moved through the forests, trying to avoid large bands of colonists and Indians who were looking for him.

He headed back toward the peninsula and his burned-out village of Pokanoket. He knew by now that he was going to die and he wanted to die in the homeland.

The handful of Wampanoags still with him knew it was the end, also, and one of their number suggested that he give himself up.

Angered, Philip had the man put to death. The Indian's brother, a brave by the name of Alderman, deserted and went over to the whites.

On August 11, 1676, a band of forty Englishmen, some Sakonnets, and Alderman, the Wampanoag brave, crossed over to the peninsula where the war had begun.

Philip and his few remaining braves were sleeping in the brush shelters when the party surrounded them, opening fire. The Wampanoags tried to make a dash into the swamp. Alderman shot Philip before he could reach the water.

King Philip's War was over after a bloody and costly year of fighting. The first real attempt by an Indian alliance to turn back the white tide had failed. The power of the New England tribes had been broken, and never again would they rise to resist the white men who, foot by foot, and yard by yard, took over their lands.

Philip was dead, almost within sight of the village in which he'd been born. Others would take up the gauntlet—Pontiac, Tecumseh, Sitting Bull, Chief Joseph, Crazy Horse, and many, many more. The pattern had been established; the die had been cast. Through the long years ahead the conflict would continue.

PONTIAC

[1720-1769]

Two miles downstream from Fort Detroit on the Detroit
River at the Potawatomi village, bands of Ottawas, Hurons,
and Potawatomies were gathered in a great council, listening
to the powerfully built, forty-year-old Ottawa chieftain Pontiac speak.

A tremendous orator with a strong ringing voice, he was
dressed in deerskin leggings, breechcloth, a few feathers
twisted in his black hair. There were silver bracelets on his
arms, some beads in his earlobes, and a ceremonial stone
through his pierced nose.

"It is important, my brothers," Pontiac was saying to the
council, "that the exterminators of our land and our people,
whose only aim is to destroy us, be stopped. You and I can
see that we no longer can supply our needs as we used to do
with our brothers, the French. The British charge us twice
as much as the French did and their goods do not last. . . .
No sooner have we bought the blanket then we must get another. . . . When we leave for our winter camp they will not
let us have anything on credit. When I visit the British chief
and tell him that some of our comrades died he does not ex-
press sorrow as did our brothers, the French. . . . They
make fun of us. . . . If I ask for something for our sick he re-

19

fuses and says that he has no use for us. It is clear from all this that they want to ruin us. My brothers, we must fight and we can win. They are few and we can win easily. All the nations that are our brothers are ready to attack them. Shouldn't we strike? Are we not men like them? Have I not shown you the wampum belt our Great Father the King of France gave to us? He tells us to strike. Should we not listen to his words? What do we fear? The time has come. . . . After the British are defeated we will see what we shall do and we will bar every way that leads to our country."

It was a powerful speech and Pontiac's own Ottawas, the Hurons, the Potawatomies, listened carefully. In this spring of 1763 other tribes were listening, too, tribes to the south, to the west, and east.

The British had been pushing at the Indians from every direction since 1759, a year of disaster for the French in America. With the exception of the Iroquois Federation, most midwest tribes, and most frontier tribes, had no use for the British.

The French they liked. The French were friendly. They had not come to take possession of the land but to trade. The French had settled along the rivers and the Great Lakes; they'd intermarried with Indians; they'd dealt fairly with them, giving them credit when credit was needed. The Indians had had guns and ammunition, and traps with which to catch the furred animals.

The British were a different breed, altogether. To begin with, General Jeffrey Amherst, in command of all British troops in America, had no particular use for Indians and forbade his men and officers to have any social contact with them.

The usual problem, though, was over the land—the great forests which Pontiac's Ottawas and the other tribes had roamed freely for generations.

The land was a gift of the Great Spirit; no man could for-bid others to enter, hunt, or plant corn on it. The Indians were accustomed to sharing what they had with all others. The principle of private ownership was completely alien to them; indeed, repugnant. In bad times the Indians gave to each other. They thought that the British at Fort Detroit and other posts in the territory should do the same.

Pontiac had fought against the British all through the French and Indian War; his Ottawas had been in on the dis-astrous attack against the redcoats under General Edward Braddock in that first real encounter of the war. He had con-tinued to fight until Fort Detroit capitulated and the post had been occupied by the British in 1760.

At first the tribes had tried to live in peace with the Brit-ish. But now Pontiac was unhappy, and the tribes around the Great Lakes, along the rivers, all the way to Pennsyl-vania, were listening. The British had to be driven out of the land. There would be an attack on all British settle-ments. It was to begin at Fort Detroit.

Instead of rushing at the fort in an outright attack, the new Indian federation had worked a clever stratagem in its planning. Still outwardly friendly to the British at the post, Pontiac and his warriors had offered to put on a dance for the entertainment of his white "friends."

While some of the young men were whirling and stamp-ing in the Calumet Dance, a few of the braves were moving about the post, examining the defenses, the cannon emplace-ments.

Now, in the spring of 1763, Pontiac was ready to open hostilities, and in a hundred villages around the Great Lakes, through the northwest frontier, other red men were waiting, too—the Miamis, the Delawares, the Shawnees, even the Senecas, part of the Iroquois League. They were listening in the villages of the Sauks, the Chippewas, the Hurons, the Mingos. Pontiac, the Ottawa, was ready to begin.

He'd been raised in this country in a village of bark-covered cabins similar to the Iroquois longhouses. In these woods he'd hunted and trapped bear and beaver, fox and otter, with guns and ammunition and traps provided by the French. He'd come to know the French settlers and traders around Fort Detroit, and they had now convinced him that if he could arouse the tribes and hit at the British posts throughout the country, the French king would most certainly send help and aid.

Relying on these promises, Pontiac went to war.

Because he'd inspected the defenses of Fort Detroit and knew that a frontal attack against British cannon was suicidal, he drew up his plans to get inside the post on a friendly visit with the British officers and then wipe them out in a surprise attack.

Accordingly, he asked for a council with the commanding officer. Some of his Ottawa braves were to accompany him inside the post, carrying knives and tomahawks and sawed-off muskets under their blankets, while the rest of his warriors were to be ready outside when the gates were thrown open.

The British commanding officer, however, had been warned of this treacherous plan by a Chippewa girl by the name of Catherine, who, it was said, was in love with the officer.

At any rate, the British were ready when Pontiac and his warriors entered the post. The shops were closed, everything was locked up, and the entire garrison was lined up on the parade grounds, muskets in readiness.

Chagrined, Pontiac said to the commanding officer, "We

are greatly surprised, my brother, at this unusual thing you have done to have all the soldiers under arms. . . . Some bad bird has given you news of us . . . to stir you up against your brothers, the Indians."

The signal agreed upon by the Ottawas for the attack inside the post was that Pontiac, who was carrying a wampum belt with the white side facing the British major and the opposite green side facing the Ottawas, was to turn the belt around.

Seeing the British soldiers drawn up in battle array, Pontiac wisely called off the fight. He presented the belt as planned, except that he did not turn it.

He had other plans, though, and he came again with his Ottawas for a general friendship council, resolved that this time they would really begin the war when the British commander opened the gates.

Again, however, the British thwarted him by refusing entry to more than a few of the men at a time. Pontiac went back to his village and began hostilities immediately.

Fort Detroit was surrounded. Small parties of the British outside the post were killed, and some flatboats carrying supplies to the fort were captured.

War belts carried the message to all the tribes down in the Ohio Valley. The red allies hit at Fort Sandusky in northern Ohio, at Fort Miami in Indiana, and elsewhere. Delawares and Mingos under their war chief, Wolf, roamed up and down the Monongahela Valley. They laid siege to Fort Pitt.

Fort Pitt, with a strong garrison, held off the red attacks, but the other posts fell one after the other. At Fort Detroit the British, unable to leave and unable to bring in reinforcements at first, were in a bad way.

Outside the post Pontiac moved with his Ottawas, stopping all supplies from reaching the garrison. He assumed that now that he'd started the war, the French traders in the vicinity would give him support. There was still a French fort in Illinois and Pontiac looked for French soldiers and cannon to assist him.

Already, though, in faraway Paris, British and French negotiators were sitting down at a peace conference to settle their differences without thought of red men on a distant continent beginning new hostilities.

At Fort Niagara on Lake Erie it was a very real war. The Indian allies struck at a line of flatboats carrying munitions to Niagara, with Pontiac, having switched his attack from Fort Detroit, leading them. The boats had been pulled up on the beach for the night. In the surprise attack the Indians captured most of the cargoes.

On the northern tip of Lake Michigan at Fort Michillimackinac the Chippewas and Sauks were having a game of lacrosse, with the British soldiers watching the contest. The Chippewas and Sauks were supposed to be friendly Indians.

Some Indian women moved past the sentries, coming supposedly to trade but with knives and tomahawks hidden under their blankets. Then one of the lacrosse players hooked the ball over the wall of the stockade and into the fort.

The players rushed after the ball. Then, dropping their lacrosse sticks, they snatched the knives and tomahawks from the women and began attacking the garrison, while hundreds of other Indians who had been watching the game rushed in also, capturing the post.

The Senecas, former allies of the British, joined the Indian federation and hit at Fort Mingo and Fort LeBoeuf, destroying both posts, and then, with Pontiac leading them, captured Fort Presque Isle.

A large band of Shawnees, Delawares, and Mingos were

still besieging Fort Pitt with its 300-man garrison. Inside the post there had been an outbreak of smallpox.

The Indian allies around Fort Pitt sent in two Delaware chiefs to discuss with the commanding officer the surrender of the fort, telling him that all the British posts to the north had been destroyed, and that a great Indian army was on the way east.

The commanding officer thanked the chiefs for their warning and presented them with two blankets and a handkerchief, objects taken from smallpox patients. Very shortly a smallpox epidemic raged through the besieging Indians around Fort Pitt. About six years earlier the Ottawas themselves had carried smallpox back to their tribe when they had attacked the soldiers sick of the disease after the surrender of Fort William Henry on Lake George.

As usual in Indian warfare, there were atrocities on both sides. The allies of Pontiac, when raiding a settlement, put all to the tomahawk, men, women, and children. Forts that were taken were burned and the inhabitants killed. Captives died by dreadful torture.

General Amherst's orders were that all Indian prisoners were to be put to death, and he suggested that the army "contrive to send the small pox among the disaffected tribes of Indians," thereby condemning women and children to miserable deaths in their lodges.

A reinforcing party of 260 men managed to reach Fort Detroit by water, coming in under cover of a heavy fog. Considerably stronger now, the British slipped out of the fort to hit at Pontiac's camp at dawn, hoping to break the siege.

French settlers, however, had warned the Indian chief of the raiding party from the post and he was ready for them. He'd already sent his women and children away from the village and had 250 of his braves waiting in a wooded area about a mile from the fort.

The British were crossing a small bridge over a creek when the Ottawas hit them from all sides. Troops rushed across the bridge, dislodging the few warriors ahead of them, but when firing broke out in their rear they realized that they'd walked into an ambush.

The British commanding officer tried to turn his men around and get back to the post, but by now Pontiac's braves were dug in behind him. A large party of them were in the excavation of a Frenchman's house, blocking the British retreat.

When the British finally stormed the Indian position, the commanding officer was killed by an Indian bullet. The remainder of his troops made it back to the post but they'd had twenty killed and forty wounded.

More reinforcements, though, were getting into Fort Detroit from Fort Niagara on Lake Erie. Back at Fort Pitt, the other besieged British post, the defenders awaited Colonel Henry Bouquet who was on his way west with reinforcements.

Breaking through a strong party of Delawares, Mingos, Shawnees, and Hurons, Bouquet reached Fort Pitt, raising the siege.

Unable to breach the Fort Detroit defense, Pontiac turned his attention to the source of supply, Fort Niagara on Lake Erie. Ordinarily, supplies from the east were unloaded at the bottom of the falls, with wagons carrying munitions and food up a narrow, winding road to the top where the supplies were transferred to boats and taken westward across the lake and down the chain of lakes to Fort Detroit.

A large Indian party struck at one of these wagon trains on the road between dense woods and a cliff wall. When the screeching red men charged, tomahawks in hand, and fired their muskets, panicked horses and oxen plunged over the precipice, drawing soldiers with them.

When two companies of British troops came out from Fort Niagara to rescue the wagon train they were ambushed a mile away, and eighty men were killed.

As usual, though, with the war dragging on this long summer, the Indian allies grew tired of it. Pontiac, the Ottawa, was fighting a white man's war—sieges, planned marches. It was continual warfare with no time for the Indians to plant corn, squash, and melons. They had little time to look for meat.

Braves from the villages in the vicinity of Fort Detroit slipped away to hunt. Some of the chiefs even held councils with the British commanding officer, offering peace behind Pontiac's back.

Even the French settlers in the area, convinced that Pontiac couldn't win in this fight, surreptitiously brought in much needed supplies to the British.

Again and again Pontiac appealed to his red allies to continue the war. He called a grand council, pleading with the chiefs to support him, but winter was coming on and there was no food. There was no ammunition for the guns because the French traders, believing that Pontiac would lose, had switched allegiance.

In October, Pontiac received word that the French and the English had signed a peace treaty, that there was no war between them, and that the Indian nations were to bury the hatchet.

Pontiac, realizing that it was impossible to continue the siege of Fort Detroit, sent a note to the British commander:

My *brother*. The word which my Father has sent to make peace I have accepted. All my young men have buried their hatchets. I think you will forget the evil things which have been taking place for some time. Likewise, I shall think of nothing but good. I, the Chippewas, the Hurons, we will speak with you whenever you ask us to.

Pontiac then moved with his Ottawas to spend the winter on the Maumee River. Farther east, though, some Indian allies were still on the warpath. A Seneca warparty hit at Fort Niagara. Huron and Miami bands were still making raids on the settlements.

In the spring Pontiac went west to try to rally the tribes along the Illinois River but was unsuccessful, just as he'd been unsuccessful in his peace overtures to the British. He tried to get ammunition from the French posts in Illinois, but was refused.

There were more defections. Colonel Bouquet forced the Delawares and Shawnees to sign a peace treaty. Finally, Pontiac capitulated, too. There was one condition he insisted upon, however. He wanted it distinctly understood that the British at the forts would not bring settlers into the country.

He insisted, from his very weak bargaining position, that the country belonged to the Indians and that the British were there simply to trade. The British representatives agreed to this request.

As the spokesman for the Great Lakes tribes, Pontiac attended a peace conference in Oswego, New York, in 1766. Here the British agent, Sir William Johnson, gave him special consideration. Pontiac, who had started the rebellion in the first place, was even receiving a pension from the British!

His own tribe turned against him. With a few friends, he left the Ottawas, moving to the Illinois country which was still French. A Peoria Indian with whom he was traveling knocked him down with a club and stabbed him to death.

The year was 1769.

The murder was supposed to be in revenge for some act by Pontiac against the Peorian Indian, but there were many who claimed that the Ottawa chieftain had been put away by the British. He'd been a thorn in their sides for too many years.

At one time he'd had eighteen different Indian tribes fighting with him against the British. Over four hundred British soldiers, and hundreds upon hundreds of settlers, had been killed in the fighting, and for a while British control over the Great Lakes country from Ontario to the Mississippi had been broken.

The British Government, however, not wanting another bloody conflict like the Pontiac Rebellion, had decreed in October, 1763, that there would be no more settlements west of the crest of the Appalachians and that the land beyond the mountains would remain *forever* Indian country.

By 1776, though, white men east of the Appalachians were no longer English but American and therefore not subject to British decrees. Men like Daniel Boone and scores of others were moving through the mountain passes into the lush lands beyond. The push westward continued.

JOSEPH BRANT

[1742–1807]

THE DRURY LANE THEATER in London, England, in the year
1786, was the nation's most distinguished playhouse, and on
this particular evening Shakespeare's *Romeo and Juliet* was
being presented to its usually distinguished audience.

Among the spectators in one of the boxes sat a rather unusual personage. He was dressed in the clothing of the
period—coat of plum-colored velvet, ruffled white shirt,
laced cuffs, short trousers tied at the knees, and silver-buck-
led shoes. On his head, though, instead of the wigs worn by
others in the audience, the dark-skinned gentleman with the
high cheekbones and flashing black eyes wore a colored turban.

Many of the spectators nearby thought at first that he was
a prince from India, but soon the word spread that the man
in the turban was the famous Thayendanegea, or Joseph
Brant, a Mohawk Indian from America.

The Mohawk chief, Brant, sat erect, his dark eyes following the movements of the players on the stage, listening to
Shakespeare's immortal words and understanding them per-
fectly, because he spoke English fluently. In the course of his
lifetime, Brant was twice presented to King George the
Third of England.

This Indian from America was completely at ease at court or in the box at the Drury Lane Theater. James Boswell, biographer of Samuel Johnson, toured London with the Mohawk chief and asserted in one of his many journals that "Captain Brant was a gentleman."

The German and English settlers, however, in the Mohawk Valley in central New York had quite a different conception of Joseph Brant, who held a captain's commission in the British Army. For years, Thayendanegea had led his band of warriors up and down the Valley, burning, killing, leaving behind mile after mile of ruined cabins and farms.

On the New York frontier during the American Revolution the name Brant was a synonym for "devil" to the settlers. Allied with the British forces operating out of Canada, Joseph Brant had proved to be what Lord Jeffrey Amherst proclaimed him—"England's finest ally."

To begin with, Brant was a member of the strongest, most warlike tribe of the Iroquois Confederacy. The lands of the Iroquois stretched through central New York, along the banks of the Mohawk River and on out along the Great Lakes. The area of their lands was shaped roughly like the longhouses in which they lived. The Mohawks, the most easterly tribe, were the guardians of the Eastern Door. Next came the Oneidas, and in the center were the Onondagas, keepers of the sacred council fire of the Iroquois. The Cayugas came next, and the Senecas occupied the most westerly lands and were the keepers of the Western Door of the Iroquois longhouse. The displaced Tuscaroras applied for a position in the Confederacy, originally the Five Nations, and, under the patronage of the Oneidas, were admitted into the League, which became known as the Six Nations of the Iroquois.

Joseph Brant had not been born in the Mohawk Valley but down along the banks of the Ohio, about the year 1742. The Ohio, then, was a hunting preserve for the Mohawks and the other Iroquois tribes which roamed far and wide during those years when the French and the English were trying to establish supremacy in the lands beyond the Appalachians.

Who the natural father of Thayendanegea was remains in some doubt. The boy was about six years old when his mother brought him back to the homeland, along with another son and an older daughter by the name of Degonwadonti. The mother married a much respected Mohawk chief by the name of Aroghyidecker, or, as he was known by the settlers, Nichus Brant. Joseph and his sister, called Molly, accepted the name of their stepfather.

These names are easily explainable. A great many Mohawk children in those years before the American Revolution were given second, English or Germanic names by the settlers. The Mohawks had been living in close proximity to these settlers for generations.

They were no longer a primitive people, depending upon hunting or fishing for their livelihood. Their towns in many cases consisted of groups of bark-covered houses surrounded by wooden palisades. It was these palisades which caused the early settlers to call the Mohawk towns "castles." The Indians cultivated the fields; they raised livestock—horses, cattle, poultry—and were well acquainted with their white neighbors.

In the Mohawk territory about twenty miles to the west of Schenectady lived William Johnson, an Irishman in the service of the Crown. He had settled there as a trader in 1738, and in 1743 had been appointed to the post of Superintendent of Affairs of the Six Nations by the British.

Every Indian on the New York frontier knew William Johnson during those years before the outbreak of the war between the French and the English for possession of a continent. Unlike many other British traders and agents, he was a fair-minded man, never breaking Indian laws, dealing justly with them in their transactions. He learned the language; he was adopted into the Mohawk tribe at Canajoharie, the Upper Mohawk Castle, by the great chief Tiyanoga, called King Hendrik.

Across the river from the Lower Mohawk Castle, Teantontalogo, William Johnson had his trading post and home. Living close by the estate of William Johnson, Joseph became acquainted with the half-breed son of the agent, Tagchuento, called Little Will. The two became close friends, a friendship which was to endure for life.

Joseph's sister Molly, a very attractive girl, soon caught the eye of William Johnson, who sent her to a school for young ladies in Schenectady. When she returned he married her, making Joseph Brant his brother-in-law.

There was one trait of William Johnson's which at first had rather amused the Mohawks. William Johnson liked to own land, and he was constantly engrossed in the business of adding to his already vast possessions along the Mohawk River.

Why William Johnson wanted more and more wilderness tracts along both sides of the river the Indians could not understand, because they knew he could never in a lifetime make use of all that land.

Shortly, though, the Mohawks discovered that not only did William Johnson want land but that every white man coming into the country seemed to have but one thought in mind—the acquisition of land—and this had begun to bother the Mohawks. The new landowners naturally forbade the Indians to plant crops on their property. It became evident that sooner or later these land acquisitions by the whites would cause trouble.

Through the influence of his sister, Joseph was sent to a settlement school in Canajoharie, where he learned to read and write. This was not too unusual, as a great many Mohawks, with the help of missionaries brought in by William Johnson, could read and write to some extent. In fact, the First Free School in the State of New York was established in Johnstown by William Johnson in 1764.

At the age of thirteen, when hostilities broke out between the French and the English, Joseph Brant had the hair plucked from each side of his head, leaving a narrow roach down the middle. He became a warrior, tomahawk and knife in his belt, carrying a white man's musket. He joined his brother-in-law, William Johnson, who led British armies, and the Iroquois, against the French and their Indian allies from Canada. Thayendanegea shortly began to make a name for himself as a brave and resourceful fighter.

William Johnson had been appointed Indian Commissioner in April of 1755 by General Edward Braddock, and the following year was reappointed Commissioner for the North. He was instrumental in keeping the Iroquois on the side of the English and, later, out of Pontiac's Conspiracy.

The Mohawks with William Johnson fought with a ferocity and bravery seldom seen in Indian warfare. The French and Indian War, with Indian tribes fighting on both sides, was a peculiarly bitter one. The French and English set their Indian allies upon each other. There were terrible massacres, atrocities.

Returning home to the Mohawk Valley at the conclusion of the war, William Johnson was knighted because of his invaluable services to the Crown. Joseph Brant discovered that more and more settlers had moved in—more Germans and Dutch who built solid stone houses, more settlers from New England.

Despite treaties with the Iroquois Federation establishing a line which no settlers were to cross, the settlers still came, and no real attempt was made by the British or colonial authorities to keep them out.

The young Joseph Brant was not at first particularly alarmed. His brother-in-law, who looked upon him almost as a son, sent him to Moor's Indian Charity School in Lebanon, Connecticut, along with his own son, Little Will. Here, under the direction of the Reverend Eleazar Wheelock, Joseph learned Latin, became a Christian, and a student of the Bible.

When he returned from Moor's School several years later, Joseph was made chief interpreter by Sir William Johnson in his dealings with the various tribes. Sir William gave him a salary of eighty-three pounds per year and expenses, and allowed him to live at Johnson Hall, when that beautiful building was erected in 1762. The Baronial mansion was flanked by two stone forts or blockhouses, one of which, along with the Hall, is standing today. The Indians who came to see Sir William camped across from the Hall, and a stand of locust trees in front was the site of many Indian councils.

Joseph enjoyed his work, acting as secretary for Sir William, greeting visitors, conducting business for him. Very shortly he became an influence with most of the tribes of the Iroquois League.

An Oneida girl, daughter of a chief, attracted Joseph's attention. When they were married, there were two ceremonies, the tribal wedding and an Anglican ceremony.

But Joseph's wife died, it was said of the white man's disease, tuberculosis, only a few years after the marriage, leaving a son, Isaac, and a daughter.

Shortly thereafter Joseph married her sister, who eventually died of the same sickness. Although he was still working as agent and representative for Sir William at Johnson Hall, he had begun to build himself a fine house at Canajoharie, where he tilled a hundred-acre farm and raised horses and cattle. In a fine suit of blue broadcloth, Joseph Brant at age twenty-two greeted visitors, Indian and white, missionaries, government officials, and tribesmen from the Iroquois Federation.

The Reverend John Stuart, an Anglican minister, visited him often, and the two men, red and white, worked on a translation of the Acts of the Apostles into the Mohawk tongue.

Constantly, as Sir William's representative, Joseph tried to solve the many difficulties arising between white settlers and the tribes of the Six Nations.

The difficulties, naturally enough, were over land disputes. Settlers were still moving in, going far beyond the demarcation line. Even in the Mohawk Valley there were unscrupulous land dealers taking over Indian lands for a pittance.

Acting as agent and peacemaker, Joseph now had firsthand knowledge of what was happening to his people who'd been living in the Valley for generations. Because of the increasing tension between red man and white, Sir William in July of 1774 called for a council of Indian delegates at Johnson Hall.

Representatives of many western tribes came to the great council, camping opposite the Hall, sitting on Sir William's lawn. He spoke to them earnestly, these people who had always loved him and respected him. He sought to keep the peace.

In the middle of the council, as Sir William was addressing his Indian friends, he suffered a stroke. As he was dying, his last words to Thayendanegea were, "Joseph, control your people."

In the early 1770's it had become apparent that sooner or later there was going to be trouble between the British and their colonies in America. Already, the Oneidas and the Tuscaroras were listening to the colonial representatives, and pressure was being brought upon Joseph Brant and the Mohawks to bring their red warriors into the American camp.

The once strong hand at Johnson Hall was gone. The man who'd had so much control over the Iroquois for so many years was dead. Sir John Johnson, his son by a German girl, succeeded to the baronetcy. A Tory, Sir John rallied the Tory factor in the Mohawk and was influential in keeping the Iroquois, except for the Oneidas and Tuscaroras, on the side of the English. As its colonel, Sir John led the Royal Greens, or the Queen's Own American Regiment.

Sir William's nephew, Guy Johnson, was appointed Superintendent of Indian Affairs. Guy Johnson was a lazy, shiftless man whom the Indians despised, and it was known that Joseph Brant, continuing in his position as secretary, was the power behind the throne at Johnson Hall.

When hostilities finally broke out between England and the colonies in the spring of 1775, the colonists in the Mohawk Valley captured a large supply of guns and ammunition from a British convoy. The Mohawks, realizing that the guns would shortly be used against them as British allies, retreated north into Canada. The Loyalists in the Valley, too, thought it prudent to leave, including Sir John and Guy Johnson.

Brant managed to hold most of the Iroquois Nation for the British, and it was from Canada that he and his Mohawks now operated with Sir John's regiment under Sir Guy Carleton, commander of the British forces in that province.

While the early fighting of the American Revolution was taking place in New England, Brant, as spokesman for his people, was anxious to know what was to become of the Mohawks and their holdings in New York State. He presented this matter to Sir Guy and was advised to go to England to discuss it with the British government.

It was on this occasion that he met the king and the queen, and other British dignitaries. He was given some assurance that after the peace with the colonies his Mohawks could return to the Valley and their rightful land.

The British were very anxious to keep the Mohawks fighting on their side in this bitter battle with the colonists. Sailing for New York City, which was held by the British during most of the war, Brant met with Lord William Howe, commander-in-chief of the British forces in America. He then went back to Canada to rally his Mohawk warriors and to lead them down against the settlements in the Valley.

There were no Mohawk Indians left in the Valley. Even Molly, Sir William's widow, had had to leave Johnson Hall and take refuge in Canada. American militia occupied the Hall.

All along the Valley were the settlements of the German, Dutch, and New England immigrants. The settlers had built their stone houses and their cabins; they'd tilled the fields and raised their cattle in peace, but all this was about to be changed. Their farms supplied grain that was of great importance to George Washington's army, and the British wanted the supply stopped.

Brant went from tribe to tribe in the Iroquois Federation, preaching the necessity for friendship with the British and inciting the tribesmen to war against the colonists. This was the only way he and his people could regain their homeland.

At Fort Stanwix in the Valley the Americans had rebuilt an old British post directly on the route to the Great Lakes and Canada.

According to a plan proposed by General John Burgoyne, new commander in Canada, a British army was to come down the chain of lakes, Champlain and George, and then down the Hudson past Albany to New York City, splitting the colonists into two parts.

As part of Burgoyne's plan, Lieutenant Colonel Barry St. Leger was to swing in from the west from Oswego on Lake Ontario and strike at Fort Stanwix and the Mohawk Valley settlements, joining up then with Burgoyne in the triumphant march to the south. Sir John Johnson accompanied St. Leger who had under his command four hundred regulars, six hundred Canadian volunteers, and over a thousand Indians led by Joseph Brant.

When the small detachment of colonials at Fort Stanwix learned that St. Leger's force was coming east, they sent out a hurried call for aid. An army of over one thousand settlers, all inexperienced as Indian fighters, was raised and led by General Nicholas Herkimer, a commander of the Tryon County militia, a respected German, long a neighbor of Joseph Brant.

General Herkimer's army marched west to the relief of Fort Stanwix and, en route, walked into an ambush set by Brant and his Indians. In a terribly bloody fight in which the Americans sustained losses of two hundred killed and two hundred wounded out of a possible seven hundred who were actually involved in the fight, General Herkimer was shot and later died at his home nearby.

The settlers, however, after the first shock of the ambuscade had passed, acquitted themselves well in the battle, under the direction of the wounded but calm Herkimer, and forced the Indians to break off the engagement, known as the Battle of Oriskany.

Fort Stanwix soon received aid from the east, General Benedict Arnold coming up with fresh colonials, and St. Leger's plan to wipe out Fort Stanwix and proceed through the Mohawk Valley was checked. He returned to Canada with his army and the Indians.

This blunting of General Burgoyne's west prong of the invasion force very definitely contributed to the British defeat and surrender at Saratoga in the fall of the year 1777.

From Canada, and then from nearer outposts, Joseph Brant now led his Mohawks and their allies in forays down into New York State. During the years 1778 and 1779 the Mohawk Valley was devastated. The flaming fall foliage often concealed the flaming war paint of the Mohawks, and outlying settlements as well as the forts were attacked.

A large party of Tories and Indians, led by Walter Butler, a friend of Johnson from the Mohawk Valley, and Brant, hit at Cherry Valley in the dead of winter, 1778. Two hundred Tory Rangers, fifty British regulars, and four hundred of Brant's Indians raged through the Valley killing over thirty settlers, men, women and children, and capturing seventy-one.

Before, Brant had been able to restrain his Indian followers in the raids into the Valley. A humane person, Brant had opposed the torture practiced by the Indians and had treated his captives well. In Cherry Valley, the Indians, especially the Senecas, got out of hand. The massacre shocked the British authorities as far away as London.

There were dozens of minor raids led by Brant, led by To-ries who had lived in the Valley and had had their homes and properties taken over by the colonials. By the year 1780 much of that formerly peaceful country had been ruined, hundreds of settlers had been killed, and General Washing-ton had sent expeditions to attack the Iroquois towns in an effort to stop the raids.

After General Burgoyne's capture at Saratoga, however, the British war effort was weakened. There were more de-feats in the south, and then in 1781 General Charles Corn-wallis, the British commander at Yorktown in Virginia, sur-rendered and the American fight for independence was over.

It was apparent after the defeat of the British in America that the Mohawks never again could lay claim to their be-loved Valley. The white settlers were there to stay and natu-rally would not soon forget the terrible warfare waged upon them by the Mohawks and their allies.

Brant, by now, was married to Catherine Croghan, half-breed daughter of George Croghan, an Indian agent and once close friend of both Brant and Sir William Johnson.

Still fighting for the rights of his Mohawks, Brant was ulti-mately given permission by the British to settle his people on the Grand River in Canada, between Lake Erie and Lake Huron, and here they were joined by some other Iroquois tribes that had been driven out of their homelands.

A solid settlement of log houses was built along the Grand, a village with a church and later a schoolhouse. Rem-nants of the once powerful Six Nations of the Iroquois set-tled here.

On September 1, 1783, Brant, still acting as spokesman for most of the Iroquois Nation, called a Grand Council at San-dusky on Lake Erie. To the Sandusky Council he invited many other delegates from the western lakes. The purpose of the council was to unite all Indians so that a strong front could be presented against any white men—British or American. Apparently, Brant had had enough of alliances.

Recognizing the power of this Indian Federation, President George Washington invited Brant to come to Philadelphia to meet with him. There the Mohawk chieftain was offered five thousand dollars to steer his Indians into a closer relationship with the Americans.

Brant rejected the offer, and other offers, one for a gift of land worth a hundred thousand dollars. He did not want anyone to influence him as far as his people were concerned. He was resolved to remain on the Grand River and prevent further encroachment by the whites.

In 1786 he made his second trip to England, raising funds with which to erect the first Episcopal Church in Upper Canada. As a zealous Christian, devoted to Christian ideals, he continued with his work of translating portions of the Bible into the Mohawk tongue.

The British had made him a superintendent of the Six Nations at Grand River and he was the official spokesman for the tribes. It was his plan that when Indians did sell land to whites the money would be deposited with the British Government, invested, and the profits used for their own good. It was a highly commendable plan.

Brant's proposal was not entirely pleasing to the British. What if the red men sold some of this land to Americans south of the Canadian border? Brant had become a little too powerful, a little too wise for the British authorities in Canada. An attempt was made to bring him down.

At a conference of petty chiefs in the year 1805, the British authorities arranged for him to be deposed as chief spokesman for the tribes and his position taken by a lesser chief. Most Indians along the Grand River, however, still regarded Joseph Brant as their leader.

At this time, too, Brant had other troubles, domestic difficulties revolving around his son, Isaac. Isaac was a grown man by now and not a very pleasant one. Like so many other Indians he had taken to the white man's firewater and had become little more than a drunkard, and a quarrelsome one.

After Isaac had been drinking heavily on one occasion he had an altercation with his father. There was a scuffle. Isaac was knocked down and accidentally killed.

Heartbroken, Brant shut himself up, retiring from all activity, until a delegation of Indian chiefs persuaded him that he still had much to do to improve the conditions of his people.

Now he gave way to neither British nor American interests. His people had to come first—his Iroquois.

The British Government granted him an estate on the banks of Lake Ontario where he died in 1807 at the age of sixty-five, one of the few great war chiefs to die peacefully.

The thriving city of Brantford, Ontario, Canada, was named after him, and a statue was erected there in his honor. The Six Nations, or what remained of them, made Brantford their headquarters.

Under some later treaties made with the Americans, a remnant of Mohawks did eventually return to New York State, to the Valley, but Brant, himself, and the major body of his Indians, remained in Canada, another displaced people, one of so many in the great march of the whites toward the west.

SEQUOYAH

[1760–1843]

THE YOUNG MEN were gathered around the crude forge that Sequoyah, the Cherokee, had set up in the shed behind his cabin, and upon which he turned out beautiful silver rings and bracelets, all in great demand among his people.

On the walls of the shed were fine sketches Sequoyah had made on bark and animal skins—pictures of deer, scenes of fighting, the hunts.

He drew sketches of his village, a village which in this year 1809 was very different from other Indian villages throughout the United States. For one thing, the Cherokees were quite advanced, living on several million acres of land in Tennessee and Georgia, and they'd been guaranteed their rights to the land in 1791 in a treaty with the United States. They'd made tremendous progress toward civilization.

The Cherokees had built sturdy houses with log walls and shake roofs; they'd even been building roads between their villages, and they were using white men's tools. As a matter of fact, Sequoyah, himself, at his forge, turned out excellent hoes, rakes, and spades which even the white settlers coveted.

The Cherokees had become farmers. They were raising livestock, organizing a democratic form of government, adopting formal laws, and later they even developed a Constitution based upon that of the United States.

In the year 1809 Sequoyah was very much interested in the "talking leaves" of the white man even though he'd never been to school. Picking up a flat stone, he made some marks on the stone and then showed the marks to the young men gathered at the forge. He stated that each mark meant a word and thus the stones could talk.

The young men laughed. Sequoyah, they thought, was very clever with his paints and his brushes, and his pictures on the walls of his shed, but he could not make the talking words. This was a truly marvelous thing, that a man could make marks on a piece of bark, or the smooth substance white men called paper, and another man could know what he said even though he was a thousand miles away.

Sequoyah thought about this, and the more he thought about it the more it intrigued him. In this year 1809, although he did not know it, there were literally dozens and dozens of Indian tribes scattered throughout the land, each one with a language of its own, but none were able to put words down on paper or bark and make them talk.

Sequoyah, the artist and silversmith of the Cherokees, decided he would do this. He began, naturally enough, by trying to make a symbol for each word, but very shortly he had thousands of symbols representing different Cherokee words. No one could ever learn and memorize all of them.

During the next dozen years he worked on this experiment, gradually discovering that words could be divided into parts, because different syllables kept recurring in many words.

After awhile he learned that with these different parts of words, signs representing the different syllables, he could put together any word. He had invented a Cherokee alphabet, probably the greatest achievement of any Indian on the continent.

For twelve years his people had ridiculed him for wasting his time with these strange markings. Some of the older tribesmen had even considered it sorcery, saying that Sequoyah was dealing in forbidden magic.

Now, like the whites around him, Sequoyah could write —on bark, on skins, on pieces of the white man's paper!

The leaders of the Cherokee Nation, many now living west of the Mississippi, on the Arkansas River, had heard of these mysterious marks Sequoyah had been making all these years and they decided in 1821 to test him.

A great crowd of his people had gathered with the leading tribesmen as he made some marks on a piece of paper. He wrote down a sentence given to him by another Cherokee.

Now a messenger carried the piece of writing to Sequoyah's son who stood a long distance off. The boy had been taught the writing by Sequoyah. When he received the paper with the writing on it he revealed the message immediately.

At first the Cherokees were awed, unbelieving, but soon Sequoyah convinced them that he had indeed made Cherokee a written language.

Now records and transactions could be kept; the Cherokees' thoughts, dreams, ideas, all could be transmitted and retained.

Immediately, the Cherokees responded, especially the younger men. Thousands of them took time from their hunting or work in the fields to learn from Sequoyah the secret of the "talking leaves."

Surely the Cherokees could be proud of this man, soon to be known as "the Master." He was to become the most respected member of his tribe.

Sequoyah had been born in the village of Tuskegee on the Tennessee River about the year 1760. His mother was Cherokee. It was claimed his father was a settler who went by the name of Guess, so that Sequoyah's white man's name was George Guess.

Like other young Cherokees he learned to hunt and to work in the fields with the cattle as his people took on the white man's ways. He'd gone beyond that, though, with his sketching and his work at the forge.

In the War of 1812 Sequoyah served with a band of Cherokees fighting with the United States Army against the British. Unlike many other southern tribes, the Cherokees had not listened to Tecumseh's call for Indian unity. Hundreds of Cherokees fought with General Andrew Jackson's army against the Creeks at the Battle of Horseshoe Bend.

But white encroachments on Cherokee territory intensified after the War of 1812. It was the old, old story, the slow pushing in from every side. White men settled on Indian lands and refused to move. In a reversal of the usual order, white men stole Indian cattle and horses.

Discouraged, many of the Cherokees voluntarily picked up and headed west before the whites took their lands from them. In the year 1818 a party of 330 Cherokees migrated to Arkansas, Sequoyah going with them. Already, a colony of his people had been established there.

It was here in a new, civilized village on the Arkansas River that Sequoyah completed the work on his alphabet.

The Cherokees were a prosperous, hard-working people. More and more of them learned to read and to write the Cherokee language taught them by Sequoyah.

On the Arkansas, though, the same old trouble began. The whites had crossed the Mississippi and again were harassing a peaceful people. Cattle were stolen; white men were settling close to Indian lands.

A delegation of western Cherokees went to Washington to ask for government intercession. Sequoyah went with the delegation as its most distinguished representative.

The Cherokees had begun to publish their own newspaper, the *Phoenix*, written partly in Cherokee, and the paper naturally aroused great curiosity and interest in the capital city.

Sequoyah was sought out. The famous painter, Charles Bird King, asked him to sit for a portrait. He was interviewed by newspaper men and invited to banquets.

After some discussion in the capital, the Cherokees along the Arkansas agreed to move once again, into the country known then as the Indian Nations, later to become the State of Oklahoma.

There were 2500 Cherokees making this second migration, leaving their homes and their farms without a fight, realizing how useless it was to resist the whites with their great armies, their cannons, their inexhaustible supplies.

Unlike the Seminoles in Florida, or the Shawnees and Indian allies of Tecumseh, or Red Cloud and Sitting Bull's Sioux of later years, the Cherokees hoped against hope that, as the white men moved westward in great droves, there would be a small place left for the red man.

In the new territory Sequoyah and the Cherokees settled down. They again built their log houses; they cleared the wilderness, planted their crops, raised cattle and hogs.

Sequoyah had become a teacher, instructing everyone he met, everyone who came to his farm. He taught them his alphabet so that they could read and write in their own tongue.

The settlement of Oklahoma kept growing in size as more

and more tribesmen from the East, continually harassed by the white men, gave up their lands and went west, joining Sequoyah's people.

The main body of the Cherokees, however, was still in Georgia—nearly twenty thousand strong. Land-hungry whites wanted their fertile lands. State and local governments put pressure on the Cherokees, trying to get them to move on. State laws were passed, stripping Indians of the few rights they possessed.

In 1830, Congress passed the Indian Removal Act which gave the President authority to negotiate with the tribes. The purpose of the bill was to persuade the red men to exchange their lands for other lands west of the Mississippi in Indian territory.

Choctaws, Creeks, Chickasaws, and Cherokees, living in Georgia, parts of Alabama, and parts of Tennessee, were herded away. This was not a war against wild savages who were raiding and scalping, but a war against peaceful farmers who owned livestock and cultivated large tracts of valuable land. Some even owned Negro slaves.

A number of the tribes gave up immediately. The others, some seventeen thousand Cherokees, men, women, and children, were rounded up by the United States Army and moved west at the point of the bayonet. Those who tried to resist were shot down along this infamous "Trail of Tears" to Oklahoma.

On the way four thousand people died of ill treatment and starvation. When the migrants reached the Cherokee villages in the Indian territory, Sequoyah, himself, and other tribal leaders did all they could to help the new ones get settled.

There was some difficulty in the beginning between the old settlers and the new, but Sequoyah, very influential now in tribal circles, helped solve the crisis, uniting the eastern and western Cherokee tribes.

The Cherokees in the Indian Nations had their schools, their roads, their cattle, even their own newspaper, the *Advocate,* which replaced the earlier *Phoenix,* and the *Advocate* was to be published till the year 1906. It was in 1907 that the Indian Nations became the State of Oklahoma, and the Cherokees were no longer an independent nation but part of the state.

Down through the years after the removal, Sequoyah worked with his people, always teaching them the language, giving guidance in tribal councils.

The Cherokee governing council, because of Sequoyah's invention of the alphabet which had advanced his people far beyond other red tribes, gave him an annual pension. Red men and white men came to his home to visit him.

He was a very old man when, in 1843, with his son, Tesse, and several others, he started southward on a long journey to Mexico where a band of Cherokees many years before had migrated. It was his intention to take his alphabet to these wanderers and try to help them.

After a hard trip the party found the Cherokee village, and here Sequoyah died.

He was not noted for his coups, nor for the enemies he'd killed in war; he was not skillful with tomahawk and knife, this quiet man of peace who had never fought against the white man. Despite the ignominies he and his people had suffered he'd done more for his Cherokees than any red man who'd ever lived. He'd given his people a written language. It had been an amazing accomplishment.

If ever a red man was deserving of a niche in the white man's Hall of Fame, Sequoyah of the Cherokee Nation is the man.

TECUMSEH

[1768–1813]

*E*IGHTY INDIAN canoes containing some four hundred painted Shawnee warriors moved slowly up the Wabash River, paddles rising and falling rhythmically as they approached the town of Vincennes, Indiana Territory.

In the bow of the lead canoe sat the tall, slender Shawnee Indian, Tecumseh, his hazel eyes riveted on the soldiers and civilians along the waterfront who were watching silently as they approached.

This was not war, even though Tecumseh's Shawnees were painted and armed; this was to be a peace conference with the territorial governor, William Henry Harrison.

At the moment, Governor Harrison sat on the porch of his fine brick mansion named "Grouseland," waiting for the arrival of this Shawnee warrior who had been causing so much trouble.

Tecumseh, as Governor Harrison knew, was much more than an Indian warrior coming with a band of his followers to attempt to iron out some of the difficulties between the red man and the white man in the Indiana Territory.

A highly eloquent orator, and probably the most able organizer the red man on the American continent had ever known, Tecumseh had roamed far and wide through all the

51

Northwest Territory, north and south of the Ohio River, far south to the lands of the Creeks and the Cherokees, and even across the Mississippi, visiting tribes there, trying to persuade them to join with him in a show of force against the encroachment of the whites.

And he had been amazingly successful. Far to the south, the powerful Creeks had heard his oratory and were ready to put on the war paint. To the north, the Ottawas, the Chippewas, the Winnebagos, and many other tribes had promised to join with him in his resistance to the whites.

Tecumseh had not even been born when Pontiac, the Ottawa, had attempted to organize these same tribes in an abortive effort to drive the British from their lands. Now it was the Americans who were doing the pushing, moving across the Northwest Territory in great droves and into the Indiana Territory where Governor Harrison had for years been buying up vast tracts of Indian hunting grounds, using threats and pressure when other methods failed.

And so Governor Harrison, an able Indian fighter who as a young man had been with General Anthony Wayne in the Ohio campaigns against hostile red men, waited at Grouseland, in August of 1810. The judges of the territorial Supreme Court were with him. A number of army officers and a detail of soldiers were nearby.

On the porch with the governor were many finely dressed ladies and gentlemen, businessmen of Vincennes and civic leaders and their wives, all here to watch Governor Harrison put the red Indian revolutionist in his place.

The group on the porch stared curiously as a small party of the Shawnees, after beaching their canoes, came up from the river toward the mansion. There was a titter of excitement from the women. The Shawnee chieftain at the head of the file of Indians coming across the grass was a fine-looking man, tall, well built, dressed in buckskins, with a feather in his hair.

The warriors stopped, refusing to come any farther. An army officer moved toward the Shawnees, indicating that Tecumseh was to come up and take a seat on the porch for the conference with the governor.

Tecumseh listened as the officer spoke to him through an interpreter, explaining what he was to do. The Shawnee shook his head and the officer stared at him in surprise.

Word went back to Governor Harrison that Tecumseh positively refused to go up on the porch but insisted upon sitting on the ground with his warriors, conducting the conference under a stand of walnut trees nearby.

Annoyed, Governor Harrison eventually had the chairs taken to the grove. He left the ladies on the porch. It was here within sight of the mansion that the two men met for the first time.

William Henry Harrison had been born in Virginia, the son of wealthy parents. As governor of the Indiana Territory he looked upon the Indians as red savages. He was decidedly unsympathetic with the claims of Tecumseh and his people who wanted to roam at will over millions and millions of acres of virgin land, land which could be put to cultivation.

To Harrison, and to so many like him in Tecumseh's day, it was utterly ridiculous that these scattered tribes of ignorant savages with "none of the natural graces God had bestowed upon the white man" should be permitted to control vast provinces. It seemed almost against the Divine Will!

The Americans had fought the French in the French and Indian War, they had fought the British in the American Revolution, and now these vast lands beyond the mountains lay open to them.

How foolish it would have been to stop now! Savage Indians inhabited these lands. The policy was to pay them a few cents an acre, to let them become assimilated or move across the Mississippi.

Governor Harrison, with the urging of President Thomas Jefferson, had succeeded in purchasing over thirty million acres of land in the Indiana Territory. Jefferson wanted the Americans to expand all the way to the Mississippi, removing the Indian tribes along the east bank.

Years before the meeting at Grouseland between Tecumseh and Governor Harrison, President Jefferson had been fearful of a French push up the Mississippi from New Orleans. The Emperor Napoleon of France had been moving his great armies all over Europe, conquering much of the continent. The French before 1803 had owned New Orleans and all that vast territory west of the Mississippi known as Louisiana. What was to prevent Napoleon from some day moving troops up the river, consolidating his claims there, and challenging the new United States of America?

The policy, therefore, of President Jefferson and succeeding United States Presidents was to expand westward—ever westward. The Indians along the east bank of the Mississippi had to be removed, legally if possible, but removed no matter how—by threats, by pressures, by bribery, by dealings with drunken chieftains who had no authority to make decisions for others.

Tecumseh now was the spokesman for those tribes which had been steadily resisting the pressures to sell and remove across the river.

The two men, red and white, took their seats in the grove, a guard of soldiers nearby, Tecumseh's Shawnees on the ground.

Tecumseh spoke first through the interpreter:

"Once, the tribes were a happy race. Now they are made

miserable by the white people who are never content but forever encroaching. The only way to stop this evil is for all the red men to unite and claim a common and equal right to the land. That is how it was at first, and should be still, for the land never was divided, but belongs to all for the use of every one. No groups among us have a right to sell, even to one another, much less to strangers who want all and will not do with less. . . . Sell a country! Why not sell the air, the clouds and the great sea as well as the earth?"

Tecumseh, the fiery orator, had more to say:

"You have taken our land from us, and I do not see how we can remain at peace if you continue to do so. You tried to force the red man to do some injury. It is you who are pushing them on to do mischief. You are trying to keep the tribes apart and make distinctions among them. You wish to prevent the Indians from uniting and looking upon their lands as common property. You take tribes aside and advise them not to come into this union. . . . Brothers, you ought to realize what you are doing with the Indians. It is a very bad thing and we do not like it."

Governor Harrison listened to the interpreter, making no comment until he was finished. Then he stated that much of the land which was now being disputed had been the possession of the Miami Indians and the government had legally purchased it from them, that the Shawnees were not really involved in the matter. He stated further that if the Great Spirit had intended for all Indians to be united he would not have given them different tongues but they would all have the same language.

Harrison asserted that the Great Father in Washington would not give back an acre of land which had been purchased legally from different tribes in the Northwest and Indiana Territories.

The interpreter had only begun to translate the governor's speech when Tecumseh, eyes flashing with rage, leaped to his feet and shouted, "What that man says is a lie!"

Governor Harrison came up out of his seat, also, drawing his sword, face red with anger when he learned what Tecumseh had said. He now stated flatly that the council was over and he told the Shawnee chief and his tribesmen to leave.

However, the next day Tecumseh apologized for his anger and then promised on behalf of his Indian allies that his people would serve with the United States in the coming war with the British if the land which had been taken illegally from his people in the Indiana Territory was restored and no further treaties were made except with the real leaders of the tribes.

Governor Harrison, of course, was in no position to renegotiate treaties or to give up lands which were already occupied by white men.

The council at Grouseland ended with no concessions made by Tecumseh or Harrison. No concessions could have been made. The courses of the two men were diametrically opposed.

As an Indian Tecumseh had no choice but to continue with his plans for consolidating the tribes, joining in with the British, and driving the Americans out of the territory.

Governor Harrison, representing the United States government, had his orders to proceed with the acquisition of Indian lands east of the Mississippi.

Tecumseh went back to the big Shawnee village on the Tippecanoe River, brooding over the injustices suffered by his people.

He'd seen much injustice since his birth in an Indian town in Ohio about 1768. When he was about seven his father had been killed by frontiersmen; his older brothers, too, had been killed fighting against the whites who were encroaching upon their lands.

The villages in which he'd lived had been raided on more than one occasion by invading armies and destroyed. There had been raids and counter-raids in Kentucky and the Ohio country. When he was about twelve years old, George Rogers Clark led an army of Kentuckians into the Ohio country, burning Indian town after Indian town, including Piqua, where Tecumseh was then living.

A chain of army posts stretched through Indian country from the Ohio to Lake Erie. The young Tecumseh had fought fearlessly with his people in battles against American armies commanded by Generals Arthur St. Clair and Anthony Wayne in 1791 and 1792. He'd learned how to handle tomahawk, knife, and rifle, and soon had become recognized as an able and competent hunter and warrior.

In the interlude of peace after the invading armies had left he saw what was happening at the trading posts in the settlements; he saw what the white man's rum was doing to many of the tribes, depriving them of their manhood.

He saw drunken chiefs put their marks on treaties which gave the white men great tracts of land. His hatred of the white man increased almost daily.

With hunting parties he traveled far and wide to the south and even across the Mississippi after buffalo. He met the Cherokees and the Creeks; he met Ottawas, Choctaws, Miamis, Delawares, Chippewas. He listened to them, and always the complaint was the same. White settlers were coming onto Indian lands. Great land companies were purchasing vast tracts of land from chiefs who had no right to sell and then were dividing the tracts into homesteads with no regard whatever for those who were already settled there in

Indian towns, growing crops.

Tecumseh bitterly resented the treaties forced upon the Indians by conquering American armies. As he traveled now he spoke to tribal leaders, pointing out the injustices of the white man's treaties, the slow but inexorable push of the settlers, with the game growing scarcer all of the time and no room left for the Indians to plant their corn and beans and melons.

He told of the frustration of finding fences across old trails, and of hunting areas now being used for pasturage for cattle, horses, and hogs.

An Indian who murdered a white man was promptly tried and hanged, but a white man who killed an Indian, even though he might be tried and convicted, almost invariably managed to "escape."

At a council in 1799 on the Mad River, Tecumseh made a great speech to the assembled chiefs, telling of the first contacts with the whites coming down the Ohio. He told of the wars and the invading United States armies under Clark, St. Clair, and Wayne.

It was a fiery, powerful speech, the speech of a natural orator who was able to hold his listeners spellbound as he talked on for hours, denouncing the white invaders.

The white men, though, were not interested in the ravings of a red orator deep in the forest. The whites moved across the Northwest Territory and into the Indiana Territory beyond, and Governor Harrison went on with his purchases of Indian lands.

But it was not Tecumseh the orator and warrior, organizer of the tribes, who first came to the attention of Governor William Henry Harrison and the white authorities in the Indiana Territory those years before the outbreak of the War of 1812.

Tecumseh had a younger brother known far and wide as "the Prophet." Like Tecumseh, he was a fluent and impassioned orator. The gist of the Prophet's message to Indians everywhere was that they were to renounce the white man's ways; the Indians were never to touch whisky; they were not to intermarry with whites; they were to wear Indian dress and eat Indian food; and if they did this, the Master of Life, the Great Spirit, would reward them with the recovery of their lands. They would be able to push the whites out of their country.

It was a kind of religious mania which swept through many of the tribes, a madness which was to be repeated in the Far West years later.

The Prophet and Tecumseh gathered around them not only Shawnees but other tribes, setting up a town on the banks of the Wabash near the mouth of the Tippecanoe River in Indiana Territory in 1808, a town of bark houses and fertile fields.

More and more tribesmen came to listen to the speeches of Tecumseh and the Prophet, and the village of Tippecanoe became known to the whites as a hotbed of conspiracy. They were a rather remarkable team—Tecumseh, the warrior, and the Prophet, the religious leader.

Tecumseh sent messengers as far as Lake Superior on the north and the Gulf of Mexico on the south. He was constantly traveling, visiting the tribes.

"Where today are the Pequots?" Tecumseh demanded of his listeners. "Where the Narragansetts, the Mohicans, and many other powerful tribes of our people? They have vanished before the rapaciousness and oppression of the white men as snow before a summer sun. In the vain hope of defending their ancient possessions they have fallen . . . the destruction of our race is at hand unless we unite in one

59

common cause against a common foe."

Hostilities seemed imminent. At Tippecanoe there were about a thousand warriors, but even these Tecumseh knew could do nothing against the power of the United States. The renewal of the war between the British and the Americans seemed inevitable. The strategy was for the red men to align themselves with the British and in this way recover their stolen lands.

On September 26, 1811, more than a year after the meeting with Governor Harrison at Grouseland, Tecumseh was on a six-month trip far to the south, visiting with the Creeks and the Cherokees, the Choctaws, the Seminoles, and other southern tribes. While he was on this trip, Governor Harrison moved toward the Prophet's town of Tippecanoe.

Taking advantage of Tecumseh's absence, as well as of an incident in which some white men had been killed by Potawatomies in Illinois, Harrison had organized a small army with the intention of presenting a show of force to the Indians at Tippecanoe. Tecumseh previously had given his younger brother strict orders not to clash with the whites, as the confederacy he envisioned was not joined as yet, and the British and the Americans were not at war.

"Wait," Tecumseh ordered.

However, when Governor Harrison's army moved close to the Tippecanoe village, the Prophet became agitated. Harrison had with him close to a thousand men, Kentuckians and Indiana frontiersmen.

The move by Harrison was not by order of the United States government. The Prophet's town was considered by all white men as an irritant, a possible source of trouble, a place where wild-eyed Indians were listening to the speeches of the two brothers, ready, perhaps, to break out momentarily with tomahawk and knife.

Harrison marched his men to within sight of the Indian village, made his camp, and began to drill his troops. It was an evocative move if ever there was one. He posted his sentries and set up his command of battle, but refrained from making the first move.

The Prophet, not a great warrior, and assuming that the Americans would hit at them the next morning, sent his men against the camp that night. Naturally, Harrison, who had proclaimed up till then that his intentions were peaceful, was ready for them.

It was not a particularly bloody battle. The Americans lost sixty-one dead, where the Indians, after breaking off the fight and fleeing, left behind them thirty or forty dead warriors, but it was a battle which undoubtedly helped make William Henry Harrison the ninth President of the United States.

In the presidential campaign of 1840, when the former governor of the Indiana Territory was running for President, the slogan used was "Tippecanoe and Tyler, too." (John Tyler was the vice-presidential candidate running with Harrison.) William Henry Harrison had gained for himself a reputation at Tippecanoe as an Indian fighter, a man who had destroyed a powerful Indian village and confederation.

The Tippecanoe village was burned when the Indians fled. The Prophet and most of the people managed to escape, but when Tecumseh returned he was furious at his brother for permitting himself to be drawn into hostilities with the whites. It is recorded that he even struck him in his anger, and it was the end of the Prophet as a power. He was disgraced, having prophesied only victory. He had promised immunity in battle, but the Indians had been driven from their village and some of them had been killed.

The Prophet moved across the Mississippi and lived with the Osages, but Tecumseh's star was still rising. As a matter of fact, the name in the Shawnee language means "meteor," although Tecumseh is considered to be a corruption of the name Tecumthe, meaning, roughly, "wildcat lying in wait for prey."

After the fight on the Tippecanoe there were more minor clashes between Indians and whites until war between England and the United States was officially declared on June 18, 1812.

Immediately the Americans tried to insure Tecumseh's neutrality in the war although it was expected that he and his Indian allies would side with the British.

Tecumseh did not hesitate. The very next month he was at Fort Malden, Canada, across from Detroit. An American army under General William Hull, an inferior and cautious commander, was on the way with three thousand men, heading toward the post.

Tecumseh's men at Fort Malden were joined soon by the able English leader General Isaac Brock with additional troops. The combined force sent General Hull scurrying back to Fort Detroit.

Now the forces of General Brock—British regulars, Canadian volunteers, and Indian allies—besieged Fort Detroit. The American army inside the Detroit fortifications was considerably stronger than the British army outside, but General Hull did not know this.

In a very clever ruse, Tecumseh marched six hundred of his Indians across a clearing three times in succession, giving the Americans the impression that thousands of Indian allies were coming into the battle.

Fearful of an Indian massacre if the post were overrun, General Hull surrendered, to the consternation of his men and officers.

Unlike many other red chieftains, Tecumseh was a humane warrior. He was violently opposed to torture and the killing of prisoners. On several different occasions when he found some of his Indian allies trying to slaughter defenseless prisoners he angrily intervened.

All through the War of 1812 he permitted no plundering of captured towns, nor the massacre of captured settlers. Once when his warriors needed meat he came across a boy working a field with two oxen. Instead of killing the boy and taking the oxen, he took the oxen and promised the boy British money for them. When a British agent tried to renege on the promise Tecumseh made the man pay.

After the outbreak of the war and the capture of Fort Detroit, Tecumseh went south to persuade the Creeks to rise up against the Americans, and he was successful in his venture. The powerful Creek Confederacy was ultimately crushed by General Andrew Jackson, but not before doing great harm to the American cause.

General Isaac Brock, who immediately perceived the tremendous value of Tecumseh as an ally and Indian leader, had appointed him a brigadier general in the British Army, but soon General Brock was killed in action and his successor, General Henry A. Proctor, was a man of another caliber.

Although contemptuous of Proctor, who was as ineffective and as cautious as General Hull, Tecumseh was forced to fight on his side. He had an army now of nearly three thousand Indian warriors, while Proctor, the British commander in western Canada, had considerably less men with him.

William Henry Harrison, now in command of the American forces, was in Fort Meigs. The combined force of Indians and British attacked the post. Reinforcements were sent to Fort Meigs by the Americans, but Tecumseh's Indians intercepted the reinforcing column, killing 480 and taking 150 prisoners.

The prisoners were under British guard when the blood-crazed Indians began to massacre them. General Proctor made no attempt to stop the slaughter, but when Tecumseh heard what was going on he raced in among his Indians and stopped the killings, telling Proctor to his face that he was a squaw and unfit to command.

Naturally, the relations between the two men worsened. Tecumseh was fighting for a homeland, assuming that with the defeat of the Americans his people would be allowed to return to their country.

Proctor was a British officer, not particularly interested in claims, glad only that the Indians were fighting with him and not against him.

The tide of war, at first so propitious to the British, soon turned. Commodore Oliver Hazard Perry defeated the British fleet on Lake Erie, and Proctor, knowing that his small force had no chance against the Americans, decided to move his army eastward to join the main British forces there.

Angered at this apparent desertion by the British, Tecumseh said to General Proctor, "We are sorry to see that you are getting ready to flee before you even have sight of the enemy . . . like a fat animal that carries its tail on its back, but when frightened drops it between its legs and runs. . . . You have the arms and the ammunition which our Great Father (the British King) sent for his red children. If you have any idea of going away give them to us and you may go and welcome."

General Proctor was evasive, maintaining that he would still be in the fight against the Americans while retreating eastward. General Harrison's army of 3500 men was now in pursuit of the retreating British and Indian force.

King Philip of the Wampanoags, son of Massasoit

Museum of the American Indian, Heye Foundation

Tecumseh of the Shawnees, who headed a powerful Indian confederacy

New York Public Library

Sequoyah of the Cherokees, a man of peace, gave his people a written language.

Osceola of the Seminoles, who was captured under a flag of truce

Sitting Bull of the Hunkpapa Sioux, probably the best known of all Indians

Joseph Brant, or Thayendanegea, of the Mohawks, who lived to govern his people in Canada for many years

Smithsonian Institution National Anthropological Archives,
Bureau of American Ethnology Collection

Crazy Horse of the Oglala Sioux, who has become a legend. This photograph is not authenticated.

Pontiac, fierce warchief of the Ottawas. This portrait was painted by Jerry Farnsworth. No authentic representation of Pontiac is known to exist.

Chief Joseph of the Nez Percé, who wanted only to live in peace in his homeland

Proctor with seven hundred soldiers and over a thousand of Tecumseh's warriors retreated to the Thames River in Ontario, with Tecumseh constantly chiding him to stop and fight, even though Harrison's army outnumbered them nearly two to one.

On October 5, 1813, Harrison's army crossed the Thames, moving along the north bank of the river in pursuit of the British and Indians.

By now Tecumseh was practically in command of the retreating army instead of Proctor. It was Tecumseh who stood before General Proctor with a rifle in his hand and made him give battle to the Americans.

Forcing Proctor into action, Tecumseh had him line up his troops across the river road. The Shawnee chief and his warriors were stationed in a swamp just off the river.

Fifteen hundred Kentucky horsemen, all volunteer frontiersmen, charged through the British lines, swung back, and came in behind Tecumseh's Indians, as General Harrison's main army was coming up.

In the swamp Tecumseh bravely led his warriors, rallying them at every point. He was wounded again and again in the brief, bloody fight. The Indians, without ammunition, eventually had to retreat out of the swamp.

Tecumseh, the Shawnee chieftain, was not with them, though. His body, riddled with bullets, lay in the swamp. It was recovered that night by Indian friends and buried in a secret place.

It was the end of the red confederacy, the end of the British, too, even though the war was to go on for some time. The fight in the swamp on the Thames River was the end of Tecumseh's dream of an Indian Federation, and a homeland for all the tribes. It was the last time any red man would attempt to unite so many different tribes from so many different parts of the country.

At the Treaty of Ghent, which brought to a close the War of 1812, the British did make an attempt to create an independent Indian State between Canada and the United States, but the victorious Americans weren't interested in such a proposition.

American frontiersmen had fought and died for the land and they were not going to give it back to red Indians, who at some future time might again rise with tomahawk and knife to raid the settlements.

After the war Tecumseh's Shawnees were sent west to the Indian Territory of Oklahoma where so many of the other tribes had already been relocated.

The Prophet lived with the Osages across the Mississippi until his death. Previously, Tecumseh had been married to a Shawnee woman and he left a son by the name of Nathah-waynah, who was made an officer in the British Army, but who eventually went with his people across the Mississippi.

Although Tecumseh had been married to the Shawnee woman, the legend or the truth of his relationship with the white girl, Rebecca Galloway, has created considerably more interest.

Near Xavier, Ohio, lived a Scotch settler, James Galloway, a man of some education as it was said he had a library of three hundred volumes, many of them classics.

The Galloways lived close by the Shawnee village where Tecumseh was making his home some years after the American Revolution.

A rather forthright young lady, Rebecca Galloway often visited in the village and learned to speak the Shawnee tongue. She made the acquaintance of Tecumseh, the rising young brave.

Becoming close friends, Rebecca Galloway tried to teach

66

Tecumseh English and occasionally would read to him from the classics in the Galloway library.

Temcumseh, soon in love with the white girl according to the legend, asked her father's permission to marry her. The Galloways told their daughter to make up her own mind in the matter.

Rebecca accepted Tecumseh's proposal on the condition that he would adopt the white man's way of life and dress, and become a white man.

This Tecumseh refused to do because already he was having visions of his great Indian Confederacy, and living like a white man would not particularly enhance his position as a leader of the Federation.

Whether the story is true no one really knows, but it was a fact that Tecumseh was a visitor to the Galloway cabin, and the guest chair in which he sat in the home as well as the beautiful pipe he gave to Mr. Galloway are still in an Ohio museum.

William Henry Harrison, Tecumseh's arch foe who went on to become President of the United States because of his Indian victories, died one month after his inauguration.

The white settlers moved on past Harrison's beautiful Georgian mansion in Vincennes, past the burned-out Indian village on the Tippecanoe, across the Mississippi, and into the lands beyond where other red men still roamed at will but one day would have to give way before the rolling white-topped wagons and the steel rails of the white man's railroad.

OSCEOLA

[1804–1838]

GENERAL WILEY THOMPSON, Indian supervisor for the new
State of Florida, looked over the gathering of Seminole Indians. He had invited them to Fort King in north-central Florida to sign the treaty which would transport the Seminoles
to the Indian Territory of Oklahoma.

These were decidedly different Indians from others the
general had encountered north of the Florida border. Instead of buckskin, the Seminoles wore bright-colored cotton
shirts which reached below the knees; their leggings were
decorated with colored strings; on their arms and their necks
there were silver rings and amulets. In place of eagle feathers
the Seminoles wore turbans of cotton—red, green, blue.
From the turbans waved egret feathers, or white ostrich
plumes which they'd bought from traders.

Seminole chiefs were there, old Micanopy, Jumper, Cloud,
Charlie Amathla, and Wildcat. With them was the young,
handsome, well-built Osceola, not really a chieftain but already becoming very popular with the young men.

Like so many other Seminoles, Osceola had come down
from Georgia, separating from the Creek Nation years before. They were runaways; the very word Seminole, in
Creek, meant separatist.

The Creek runaways over the course of years had settled in this warm country of north-central Florida, along with some Cherokees, some Choctaws, and some bands of original Florida Indians, Calusas, all more or less united now, with the various bands having their own chieftains, but with old Micanopy looked upon as the principal chief.

Osceola was not as dark-skinned as other Seminoles. As a matter of fact, the white men around Fort King, who knew him, often referred to him by the name of Powell. It was said that his father had been an Englishman named Powell who lived in Alabama.

In the beginning, the Seminoles of northern Florida hadn't been a particular problem, even though General Andrew Jackson had been sent down from the States and had had a few brushes with them back in 1818 because of Indian raids across the border.

In 1819, when Spain sold the Florida Territory to the United States and General Jackson was made the first Territorial Governor, the land was still largely unknown to Americans. There were a few towns in the north and the northwest. There was Tallahassee, later to be the state capital, and St. Augustine, on the ocean, the largest city in Florida and the most ancient on the North American continent.

Just below these northern settlements was a land of lakes, thickets of palmetto, and swamps full of cypress trees. Still farther south lay a vast expanse of watery grasses known as the Everglades.

Shortly after the United States took over Florida, settlers moved onto the land, grabbing up as much as they could. Wealthy southern planters came in with their slaves, and there were some disputes with the Seminoles.

In a treaty, though, the tribes agreed to accept a large tract of land in southern and central Florida and to remain on that tract. But by 1828, Andrew Jackson had become President and trouble was beginning to brew.

It had begun as usual with the whites encroaching upon Seminole territory, raiding the cattle, and it was aggravated when runaway slaves from southern plantations escaped to the interior, joining up with the Seminoles.

Slave catchers came after the runaways, and the Seminoles, who treated the Negroes kindly, oftentimes tried to conceal them and help them.

Young Osceola had grown up in this atmosphere during the 1820's, living with his band in the Wahoo Swamp one hundred miles north of Tampa Bay. As was the Seminole custom, he had two wives, horses and cattle, and up till now he'd been friendly with the whites and was quite well known at Fort King.

By 1819, the year the United States purchased Florida from Spain, the Seminoles had a civilization of their own. These were not wild hunters, savages. They had been raising their own cattle; they had their cultivated cornfields; they lived in their *chickees*—thatch-roofed, three-sided huts on poles several feet off the ground.

They had been a happy people, but more and more they were becoming resentful of the whites who never seemed to have enough land, and who were constantly pushing them out.

In Washington the Indians of Florida had finally become a real problem, and the solution to the problem, as proposed by President Jackson, was to send them west of the Mississippi into the large tract of land known as the Indian Nations where other eastern tribes had already been sent.

Now it was the turn of the Seminoles. Government representatives met with the chiefs who, because of pressure or the realization that they were powerless to resist, had agreed to follow the Creeks to Oklahoma.

Naturally, most Seminoles in Florida did not wish to re-join Creek bands they'd left many years before. They liked this lush Florida country and intended to remain, but be-cause a few of the chiefs had signed the treaty, the United States transports now lay in the harbor at Tampa Bay wait-ing for the tribes to come in.

General Wiley Thompson was anxious for those who had not signed the treaty to put their marks on this new paper agreeing to the removal. He had had his desk brought out from headquarters inside the post, and the chiefs with their bands of young warriors stood nearby, faces grim.

General Thompson's treaty was quite explicit. The Semi-noles must bring in their cattle for which they were to be paid in gold; they were to give up whatever runaway slaves they had with them, and they were to be transported to Oklahoma.

Recognizing the fact that there was much dissension here, General Thompson had a pen ready and with it he wanted each chief present to make his mark on the paper.

Young Osceola stepped forward, his hunting knife clasped in his hand. Raising the knife he plunged it down into the paper on the table and shouted, "This is the only treaty I will ever make!" He turned and stalked off into the forest, the young Seminoles following him and the chiefs coming on later.

The die was cast. The main body of Seminole tribes were not going to leave Florida without a fight.

General Wiley Thompson knew this, and President An-drew Jackson, in Washington, knew it, also.

There was no fighting immediately, though. Many of the Seminoles continued to trade at Fort King. Osceola, himself, was at the post one day with one of his wives known as

Morning Dew, a slim, brown girl who was part Negro, part Indian.

A slave catcher at Fort King, seeing Morning Dew, immediately contended that she was a runaway slave and insisted upon taking her with him.

When Osceola wildly resisted, soldiers grabbed him. General Thompson, who was still angry because of Osceola's defiance of him at the treaty signing, had Osceola put in shackles as his beautiful young wife was taken away by the slave catcher.

General Thompson now tried to put pressure on the young Seminole to intercede with the other chiefs and have them sign the treaty. Osceola, in order to secure his freedom, agreed to help, but, once free, he gathered about him fierce young Seminole warriors.

They hit first at a band of their own people who had signed the treaty and were getting ready to embark on the transports. The chief and some of his followers were shot dead.

Not long after, General Thompson, walking outside the fort, was shot down, along with one of his young officers. Osceola was seeking his revenge.

By now a detachment of one hundred United States troops was marching northward from Fort Brook on Tampa Bay to reinforce Fort King. The detachment had a six-pound cannon with them and they'd been on the march for three days, the command under Major F. Dade.

The major knew by now that the Seminoles were on the warpath and he maintained a close guard. On the morning of the fourth day, though, they walked into an ambush set for them by old Micanopy and a number of others.

The entire detachment was wiped out with the exception of one survivor who was able to make it back to Fort Brook.

Only 180 Seminole warriors were in on the attack against Major Dade's force. They sustained a loss of three killed and five wounded.

The Seminoles had begun to raid in general now, hitting at farms and plantations, killing, scalping. A body of regulars and volunteers left from a small post north of Fort King to hit at the Seminole bands, particularly Osceola's young men.

In the Cove of the Withlacoochee the commanding officer of this detachment came to the river which he found quite deep with no fording place. Using an old Indian dugout canoe the men started crossing the creek. There were six hundred white men in the force which Osceola hit.

The young war leader of the Seminoles wore a green war dress with scarlet belt; black and white ostrich plumes waved from his turban headdress. With only 250 men, he defeated the whites at the ford, chasing them back to their station near Fort King.

The Seminole War raged across northern Florida. Settlers hurried into the scattered forts for protection. Rich plantation owners moved in to St. Augustine.

There were dozens of raids, quick attacks and then retreats into the swamps where it was almost impossible to follow.

Detachments of United States troops, heavily laden, cumbered with baggage wagons and packs, had no chance against this rapidly moving people. Federal troops would occasionally find a Seminole village but it was usually deserted. The villages were burned, corn fields destroyed, the herds of cattle taken. The Seminoles, themselves, moved deeper into the swamps and were as dangerous as ever.

More and more troops were sent south. General Winfield Scott, later commander of the American forces in Mexico,

73

was sent to Florida by the War Department. Then General Zachary Taylor, Mexican War hero and later President of the United States, had his try at the Seminoles in this bitter war of extinction, a war which never seemed to end.

Formal campaigns were launched, always ending in failure. But occasional bands, harassed, near starvation in the swamps, unable to plant crops, gave up and agreed to go to the Indian Nations.

Always in the forefront of the major battles and the minor raids was the young war leader, Osceola, with the black and white ostrich plumes in his turban. It was he who persuaded the older chiefs to keep up the fight.

Constant overtures of peace were made by the white generals trying to induce Osceola and the others to come in. Now some of the older men, weary of fighting and constantly hiding in the swamps, gave up. The whites were bringing in Indian auxiliaries, Choctaws, Creeks, Chickasaws, placing a bounty of five hundred dollars on a dead Seminole warrior.

It was General Thomas S. Jesup, in command of the troops around St. Augustine, who finally persuaded Osceola to talk peace. It was to be a truce, the Seminoles coming in under a white flag.

Osceola came in with seventy warriors, their wives and children, carrying a white flag on a stick. The troops closed in. To Osceola's dismay and astonishment, the Indians were marched in as prisoners to St. Augustine with great crowds gathering in the narrow streets to see them.

Through the town and over the drawbridge into the courtyard of the old Spanish castle, known now as Fort Marion, the Seminoles were taken. Here they were put into a dungeon.

Some of the young warriors with Osceola managed to escape through a high, narrow window in the dungeon. Osceola remained with the others and the women and children.

By now he was beginning to realize that it was useless to keep up the fight with the whites. There were too many of them, and they were still coming into the country, soldiers, settlers, spreading out over the land.

The Seminoles at large, outraged at the trickery, retreated farther south into the Everglades, still fighting, still resisting. At Lake Okeechobee far to the south a battle was fought against troops under General Zachary Taylor in which 26 Americans were killed and 112 wounded with only a handful of Seminoles as casualties.

Osceola, in shackles, remained at Fort Marion, but now General Jesup received orders to ship the Seminole prisoners north to Fort Moultrie at Charleston, South Carolina.

A transport carried the Seminole war leader away from Florida for the last time. His two wives and two small sons went with him.

At Fort Moultrie, situated on Sullivan's Island in the harbor of Charleston, the Seminoles were given a measure of freedom because escape was now impossible.

Osceola had become well known throughout the United States. Artists like George Catlin, who had already made a great reputation painting the Indians of the West, came to Fort Moultrie in 1838 to paint his portrait. Osceola was thirty-four years of age at this time, still a comparatively young man, but already a sick man, a sickness which may have begun far back in the swamps of Florida. His sickness may be recognized today as a quinsy throat, an infection of the throat which had made him very ill. His tonsils were inflamed and swollen, making it difficult for him even to breathe.

The Seminole leader refused the administrations of the post physician. Unable to eat, Osceola became weaker and weaker. On January 30, 1838, he made signs for his wives to bring his full dress. He put on his war outfit, painted his face, lay down on his bed robe, and died without a sound. He was buried with full military honors at the fort.

Far to the south the Seminole War continued, the young chieftains under the leadership of Wildcat, friend of Osceola. Band by band, though, they were rounded up, run down in the swamps, until only a handful remained in the deep Everglades below Lake Okeechobee.

The captured tribes were moved to the Indian territory of Oklahoma and the war was over, but at what a price!

Over twelve thousand Seminoles had been sent west from Florida and at least four thousand died on the trip. The war had cost the United States Government close to forty million dollars. Over three thousand soldiers, sailors, and marines, not counting the many white settlers, had died from Seminole bullets or disease in the swamps.

A dozen generals had fought against the renegades of northern Florida. Of the many bands, now only about 150 Seminoles remained in the deep wet lands below the lake.

Unlike other tribes, Osceola and his Seminoles never signed a treaty of peace or surrendered to the United States Government, and therefore they are not given government money, although the government does provide schools and hospitals, and agricultural help.

Osceola, war leader, who was born in Alabama and who died in South Carolina, had left his mark on the country he had loved. He had fought for his people until captured under a flag of truce. He had fought until resistance was futile.

Overlooked by some who are carried away with the stories and legends of Pontiac, Tecumseh, Sitting Bull, and Crazy Horse, the Florida chieftain may truly have been America's most formidable red enemy. None had done so much damage to white forces.

CHIEF JOSEPH

[1840–1904]

For NEARLY two months this terribly hot summer of 1877, General Oliver O. Howard, sixth ranking Civil War major general, had been on the trail of a band of renegade Nez Percé Indians as they retreated across the state of Idaho and into Montana.

All the way east, that astute Indian, Chief Joseph, had outmaneuvered the force of over four hundred white troopers and infantry, leading them a wild chase through terrible mountain country over the Great Divide.

In a place known as the Camas Meadows, General Howard's weary troops and worn-out horses rested. Camas Meadows was close by Yellowstone Park. The camp was beautifully located on elevated ground which overlooked the Meadows. It was a region with lush grass for the stock, and shade for the men under the willows along the bank of a clear stream.

For the first time in many weeks General Howard's men, constantly expecting counterattacks from the retreating Nez Percé, assumed that tonight they would be able to rest in peace. The Nez Percé were far ahead of them and supposedly moving fast.

The usual guard was posted, however; horses and mules

were brought inside a rope corral, and the cavalry stock was tied to picket ropes.

General Howard assumed that the Nez Percé were too worn out to be thinking of a night attack. They were traveling with nearly five hundred women and children, over two thousand cattle, and hauling hundreds of travois containing camp equipment.

Therefore, the last thing General Howard anticipated that quiet evening in Camas Meadows was an Indian raid. But when the white men were not anticipating trouble, this was exactly the time the Nez Percé hit at them.

It was a most unusual raid on a detachment of army men in the field. First of all, Nez Percé scouts carefully approached the bivouac and crept stealthily between the pickets, and in among the mules. They cut their hobbles and removed the bell from the lead mule.

Now one of the sentries on duty was alerted by a body of horsemen, some forty in number, riding in column of fours, advancing boldly toward the camp.

The sentries assumed that this body of men approaching in cavalry formation was a detachment of United States cavalry coming up to join General Howard's troops in the field. Several other detachments had joined the force before on this long trek after the Nez Percé.

The forty "troopers" riding in formation toward the camp were almost on top of the sentry before he identified the slim brown bodies, the feathers, the multi-colored ponies.

"Indians!" he gasped in astonishment.

Lifting his Springfield carbine, he fired into the air.

Whooping loudly, the forty young Nez Percé drove hard in among the mule herd, stampeding them, driving them out of the camp. One hundred and fifty invaluable mules, animals which had been hauling supplies for the force, were driven off. Howard accordingly had to hold up his pursuit of the fast-moving Indians to wait for more mules.

The only reason General Howard's cavalry was not put on foot was because the Nez Percé scouts in advance of the raiding party had not had time to cut the picket ropes of the cavalry mounts.

The Camas Meadows raid was just another example of the brilliant leadership and strategical maneuverings of the Indian chief who has been referred to on more than one occasion as the "Red Napoleon," the man who led one of the nation's finest generals some eighteen hundred miles across country, right up to the Canadian border, and was within one day's march of that border before he was apprehended.

It began in the beautiful Wallowa Valley of northern Idaho where young Joseph was born in 1840, the son of a chief of the Nez Percé, also named Joseph.

This friendly, highly intelligent band of Indians had occupied these mountain valleys of Idaho and Washington for generations, at peace with the white men. But like so many other tribes, the Nez Percé were now being squeezed onto smaller and smaller reservations.

The French had given them their name years before, the words "Nez Percé" meaning "pierced nose." Some of the warriors in earlier years had worn ornaments in their noses.

As far back as 1855, twenty-two years before Joseph's people broke out of the Nez Percé Reservation, they'd made a treaty with the whites, or, more accurately, *some* of the Nez Percé chieftains had made a treaty with the whites.

Old Joseph, the father, had refused ever to take his people to a reservation. He had denounced the treaty of 1855; he had refused to accept the usual annuities sent by the United States Government, and his people had continued to occupy the Wallowa Valley, a beautiful place fifty miles across and circled by mountains with forested slopes.

There were meandering streams, full of trout, running through the valley, plenty of bunch grass and sage for the horses, and there was Lake Wallowa, a gem in this mountain fastness.

This was the home of the Nez Percé. Here they raised their cattle and horses like the white men. They fished; they hunted deer and elk; and every year large hunting parties headed west for a buffalo hunt in the Crow country.

Young Joseph had a brother named Alokut, born a year later than he, who looked so much like him that many often thought they were twins.

Joseph was a big man for an Indian, 6'2" tall, weighing 200 pounds, with broad shoulders and a deep chest, very powerfully built. He had dark black hair which he wore in two braids over his shoulders and fine black eyes. In every way, he looked and acted the part of a chief.

There was a solemn dignity about the man. The whites who knew him had respect for him. He was a man of compassion, a man of peace, who knew full well the futility of fighting against the whites but who, when embarked on this course, gave them the kind of fight they'd never had before.

As a young man Joseph took to himself two wives, which was the custom with the Nez Percé. Nine children were born to the chieftain, and all died in infancy except two girls. Of the two only one lived to maturity.

The real trouble with the whites began in 1873, two years after the death of Old Joseph. Government officials by now were putting pressure on Joseph's band to join the treaty Nez Percé in the Lapwai Reservation.

Joseph's reply to the commissioners was in keeping with his character. It was the statement of a free man who'd been born free and who intended to remain free, and who resented any efforts on the part of others to tell him where to live:

"You can keep your presents; we have plenty of horses and cattle to sell, and we don't want any help from you; we are free; we can live where we want to; where we please. Our fathers were born here; here they lived; here they died; here are their graves. We will never leave them."

President Ulysses S. Grant in Washington thought differently. On June 10, 1877, he issued a proclamation throwing open the Wallowa Valley, which till then had been the exclusive property of the Nez Percé, to the whites.

For a year or two before, white settlers and ranchers had been moving into the valley, taking over land, and they were now anxious to increase their holdings. But the Nez Percé were in the way, which meant that the Indians had to go, whether or not it was legal, whether or not it was right.

White settlers brought in charges against the Indians, claiming there had been raids against their stock, claiming whites had been killed. They tried in every possible way to push the Nez Percé into acts of reprisal, hoping for an excuse to bring in the military.

A young Nez Percé was killed in a scuffle with white men, which incident ultimately brought things to a head. There were several bands of non-treaty Indians in the Wallowa Valley, Joseph's own band, another band led by young Looking Glass, and a third band led by White Bird, a fierce, warlike warrior with a terrible hatred for the whites.

In a last effort to maintain the peace, General Howard at Fort Lapwai in the spring of 1877 met with the recalcitrant chiefs, trying to persuade them to go to Lapwai Reservation.

Reluctantly, Joseph, realizing that war against the whites could result only in terrible harm to his people, agreed to take his band to Lapwai.

Looking Glass agreed to go with him, but White Bird and some of the others, especially the young warriors, fiercely refused to move and asked for war.

A handful of young bucks from White Bird's band killed several whites, and the troopers moved immediately from Fort Lapwai to apprehend them.

Joseph, now thirty-seven years of age and having had experience with the whites before, knew exactly what was going to happen. To the white soldier an Indian was an Indian, and not especially liked. As a matter of fact, a great many white soldiers stoutly maintained that the "only good Indian was a dead Indian." That included women and children, too, because "nits make lice."

Knowing that his band would be punished just as much as White Bird's band for the depredation by the young bucks, Joseph threw in his lot with White Bird.

It was the middle of June and the non-treaty Nez Percé were camped at White Bird Canyon. A hundred troopers from Fort Lapwai came to punish the wild ones.

Joseph's wife was momentarily expecting a child when the fight broke out. The Nez Percé set up an ambush, concealing themselves on the walls on both sides of the canyon as the troopers, many raw recruits, rode up.

The troops were badly mauled in the canyon, one-third of the force killed and the rest sent running back to the town of Mount Idaho, eighteen miles away.

Joseph lost two wounded in the battle.

There was no thought in the beginning by Joseph, or any other non-treaty chief, to head up toward Canada, known as the "Grandmother's Land" of Queen Victoria, where Sitting Bull, the Sioux chieftain, had taken refuge after the Battle of the Little Big Horn.

The Nez Percé wanted to remain in their homeland, close by the Wallowa Valley. Joseph, as he intimated later in his writings, hoped that they could thwart the white troopers and again get negotiations under way with the commissioners to permit them to remain.

But first of all they had to avoid the white soldiers. General Howard at Fort Lapwai immediately telegraphed for reinforcements, and five days after the battle of White Bird Canyon, Captain Marcus Miller left the fort with four hundred men to strike at the recalcitrants.

Very cleverly Joseph lured small detachments of troops into ambush and made havoc of them as he retreated toward the Clearwater River. He had less than three hundred fighting men with him and over five hundred women and children.

He had one big advantage over the white troopers—the Nez Percé had plenty of fine horses, remounts, while the troopers following them soon wore out their mounts in the terrible country of what is now northern Idaho and Montana.

At the forks of the Clearwater Joseph built rock barricades, another first for Indians on the warpath, and when Captain Miller's four hundred men assaulted them they were driven back.

The Nez Percé were dug in among the rocks on the bluff, and with Joseph leading them they fought savagely, desperately, refusing to retreat, even counterattacking, driving the soldiers back.

For two days the troopers couldn't break the line on the bluffs as Joseph's band slowly retreated in good order, heading toward the Bitterroot Mountains and the Lolo Trail.

Here began a long "Trail of Tears" for Joseph and the Nez Percé. Here, too, Joseph, always reluctant to fight against the whites, appealed to his people.

It was his intention to remain here and continue to fight rather than move east, hoping to persuade other tribes, perhaps the Crows, to join in with them.

"What are we fighting for?" Joseph asked. "Is it for *this* land? No, it is for the land where the bones of our fathers are buried. I do not want to die in a strange land. Stay here with me now and you shall have plenty of fighting."

The other chieftains wanted to move on, though, and Joseph eventually bowed to their wishes.

The Lolo Trail through the Bitterroots was a terrible hardship on Indian and white trooper alike. They moved over sheer ledges, fallen timber, rock slides, and canyons.

General Howard, who'd come up to take personal command in the chase, had with him artillery and supply wagons. On the trail of the Nez Percé he actually had to cut out roads to move his small army.

There was wild excitement as the Indians neared the town of Missoula in Montana. A white volunteer army was raised in Missoula to head off Joseph and his band. The volunteers set up a breastworks in Lolo Canyon to prevent Joseph from marching on the town, if that was his purpose.

Joseph, however, had no fight with civilians. All the way on the long march he strove mightily to see to it that no civilians were killed. His fight was with the military. Occasionally, some of his young bucks did get out of hand, though, and there were a few civilians killed, much to Joseph's regret.

The volunteer army was led by a military officer. Determined not to fight the civilians, Joseph tried to negotiate with the officer. All he wanted for his people was passage past the town of Missoula.

Unsuccessful in the negotiations, however, he calmly took

85

his band around a barricade the civilian army had set up on the side of a high cliff to prevent his passage, moved up the side of the cliff, considered impassable by the whites, and then went down into the Bitterroot Valley to the astonishment of the people of Missoula.

The maneuver left General Howard days behind him on the trail. Desperately, Howard sent word to General John Gibbon, stationed at Fort Shaw on the Sun River in northern Montana. Gibbon was to take his men and intercept the wily Nez Percé chieftain.

Still moving fast with his women, children, and stock, Joseph crossed the Continental Divide and went down into the Big Hole Valley, a beautiful land of rolling hills, dissected by streams and woods. In this refuge he set up his ninety lodges and turned out his two thousand ponies to graze. There was good forage, good hunting, and the people were quite worn out from nearly two months of constant running and fighting since they'd left the Wallowa Valley.

General Gibbon, with 150 men, a wagon train, and some civilian volunteers, suddenly appeared in the Big Hole Valley, after a quick march from Fort Shaw.

Joseph, assuming that he was temporarily safe, had for once posted no sentries, and when Gibbon's force hit them savagely at dawn they were at first paralyzed.

Retreating to a small stream bed behind the village, the Nez Percé warriors fought fiercely as usual, giving ground reluctantly. There was much hand to hand fighting with many men, women, and children killed.

When Joseph and his warriors withdrew from the village, the troopers tried to set it afire, but the abandoned lodges were heavy with dew and they were unsuccessful.

Rallying his warriors while the bluecoats were so engaged, Joseph drove the soldiers from the village, regaining possession of the Nez Percé lodges and equipment.

General Gibbon and his troopers, amazed at the ferocity of the Nez Percé counterattack, retreated among the trees. Gibbon's ammunition was low; many of his bluecoats were dead or wounded. He, himself, had been shot from his horse and was now fighting with a rifle like a common soldier. Undoubtedly, this summer day of 1877, he was having visions of another Little Big Horn.

Two of Joseph's wives were killed in the Big Hole fight, along with a daughter of Looking Glass. Out of 89 dead Indians, 70 were women and children. As usual, the bluecoats were not distinguishing between male and female.

Before Joseph and his Nez Percé pulled down their lodges and moved away from the Big Hole encampment, Gibbon had sustained losses of 31 killed and 38 wounded, out of a total of 191 troopers and volunteers in the engagement. More than a third of his force had been incapacitated in the bitter fight.

General Howard came up to join Gibbon after the engagement and his comment concerning Joseph was revealing.

"Few military commanders with good troops could have better recovered after so fearful a surprise."

At Camas Meadows, later in the month of August, the Nez Percé warriors, riding in column of fours, military fashion, ran off with 150 of General Howard's valuable army mules.

Joseph moved into Yellowstone Park with General Howard's command lumbering after him with the wagons and artillery. As Joseph entered the park a new force of white troopers joined the chase.

The reorganized Seventh Cavalry under Colonel Samuel Sturgis was stationed at the Crow Agency on the Big Rosebud River in Montana. Only a year before the Seventh had been practically annihilated by the Sioux on the Little Big Horn River.

General Howard's orders to Colonel Sturgis had been for the colonel to proceed toward the northeast boundary of Yellowstone Park and intercept the Nez Percé as they tried to pass. Now with a half-dozen companies of the Seventh, and some Crow scouts, Sturgis waited at Clark's Fork Canyon, taking a position which enabled him to guard the various passes out of the lower Yellowstone Canyon.

Once again Joseph found himself between two military forces. Very cleverly, he feigned flight down along the Stinking Water River, but, after making a short detour south, moved north toward Clark's Fork, passing through a narrow canyon where the towering cliffs were only twenty feet apart.

Moving rapidly, he came into the country of the Mountain Crows, and it was here that the Nez Percé hoped to find refuge. They were doomed to disappointment, however.

The Crows were friendly with the whites and decided to remain strictly neutral. Looking Glass had been sent on ahead for a conference with the Crows. When he came back with the bad news, Joseph realized that their only sanctuary was Canada.

Colonel Sturgis and his Seventh Cavalry, reinforced by some of General Howard's men, were still in pursuit of the Nez Percé. By now it was mid-September.

At Canyon Creek in the vicinity of the present site of Billings, Montana, Sturgis hit at Joseph's camp with 350 men. The first charge of the cavalry drove the Nez Percé back, but again they rallied, the warriors protecting the women and children who'd pulled down the lodges and were moving through a narrow valley.

In this engagement Joseph's people sustained twenty-one killed and the loss of nine hundred ponies.

Colonel Sturgis and his men kept up their pursuit of the retreating Nez Percé, but their rations were low and the men and horses worn out. At the Musselshell River they had to give up and wait for General Howard's forces.

Joseph and his band headed north now toward Canada. On September 23, they crossed the Missouri River, picking up some supplies at a freight depot which was being guarded by a handful of soldiers.

Their destination was the pass between the Bearpaw Mountains and the Little Rockies. The Grandmother's Land and safety were very close.

Unknown to Joseph, however, another army of bluecoats had taken up the chase. On the Tongue River, in Montana, General Nelson A. (Bearcoat) Miles was stationed with cavalry and infantry.

On orders from General Howard, General Miles, on September 18, crossed the Yellowstone with two troops of cavalry and a half-dozen companies of infantry to intercept Joseph and the Nez Percé.

The Indians, after eluding Sturgis' cavalry, had assumed that the fighting was over. Joseph moved his village to the northern slope of the Bearpaw Mountains, halting on Snake Creek, a tributary of the Milk River.

He was now within one easy day's march of the Canadian border, but he mistakenly assumed he was already in the Grandmother's Land. He was in a beautiful little sheltered valley which abounded with game and good grass for the ponies. Here he rested his people after the long, exhausting trek from the Wallowa.

"I sat down in a fat, beautiful country," Joseph was to say later. "I had won my freedom and the freedom of my people. There were many empty places in the lodges and in the council, but we were in the land where we would not be forced to live in a place we did not want. I believed that if I could remain safe at a distance and talk straight to the men that would be sent by the Great Father I could get back to the Wallowa Valley. . . . I had sent runners to find Sitting Bull, to tell him that another band of red men had been forced to run from the soldiers and the Great White Father, and to propose that we join forces if we were attacked."

In the meantime, General Miles was heading up toward the Milk River with 375 men, cavalry and infantry, a breech-loading Hotchkiss gun, and a 12-pound Napoleon cannon.

He reached Joseph's camp on the Milk on October 1. Cheyenne scouts with Miles were discovered by Nez Percé pony herders and the Nez Percé, who were now in the habit of digging rifle pits like white soldiers, dug pits here in front of their village.

A concerted charge by the cavalry, aided by Cheyenne and Sioux scouts, was broken by the cool, steady fire of the Nez Percé.

After the first charge the cavalry had 53 killed and wounded out of a total of 115 men. Only one officer in the battalion had not been hit.

The Nez Percé, however, were taking heavy losses, too. Looking Glass was killed, and Alokut, Joseph's beloved brother. Some of the Nez Percé lodges had been struck and a few of the band tried to escape.

Joseph had been on the opposite side of the creek from the village when the fighting broke out, but he quickly crossed the water, snatched his rifle from his wife, and got into the battle.

The Nez Percé were forced back to the ravines behind the camp. Here they again entrenched themselves, digging in with shovels made of frying pans and knives. They even dug trenches between the rifle pits and thus were able to hold off Miles' troops for five full days.

Miles' small army had completely encircled the village by now, but Miles was afraid that Joseph had been able to get word through to Sitting Bull and that the Sioux chieftain would soon be coming down at them across the Canadian border with a large body of fighting men.

Joseph's message to Sitting Bull, however, had been intercepted by some Assiniboines, enemies of the Nez Percé.

On the night of September 30, snow fell heavily, developing into a blizzard. Both Indian and white soldier suffered terribly. The troops were afraid to light fires because of the Nez Percé sharpshooters in the pits.

With his cannon, Miles now shelled the village. Both General Howard and Colonel Sturgis, learning that Miles had stopped the Nez Percé on the Milk River, hurried up with reinforcements. It was the beginning of the end.

With both sides having suffered heavy casualties, Miles started negotiations. Joseph, himself, went to the troopers' camp and had a consultation with General Miles.

The Nez Percé were starving. There were many wounded, many women and children in camp suffering, and by now General Howard had reached Miles's camp.

Joseph, realizing that it was hopeless, agreed to surrender. He said, "I am tired of fighting. . . . Our chiefs are killed. . . . The little children are freezing to death. . . . We have no blankets, no food. . . . I want to have time to look for my children and see how many of them I can find. . . . Hear me, my chiefs, I am tired; my heart is sick and sad. From where the sun now stands I will fight no more forever."

General Miles said that they would arrange to send the Nez Percé back to their own country—not the beloved Wallowa Valley but the Lapwai Reservation—but even here the white man's promise proved invalid.

Instead of to Idaho, the Nez Percé were sent down the Missouri to Fort Lincoln, near Bismarck, Dakota Territory, and then later, in spite of Joseph's protestations, they were moved to the unhealthy country of the Indian Nations in Oklahoma, where many of the people died.

Still fighting for his people, Joseph went to Washington to plead that they be permitted to return to their own land. Permission was refused until the year 1885, when a remnant of the band was finally allowed to return to the Lapwai Reservation in northern Idaho.

Joseph, himself, because there were indictments against him in Idaho for "murders" committed by his people, was sent to the Colville Reservation at Nespelem, Washington.

He was still the same dignified, quiet chieftain, highly respected by Indians and whites alike, forty-five years of age, a man whose only concern was for his people.

In the retreat from the Wallowa Valley and the long march to the Canadian border, he had fought against over 2000 American troops; he'd fought in eleven engagements; had had 150 of his men killed out of a possible 300, along with many wounded. He'd marched 1800 miles with women, children, old people, and a large pony herd and cattle. Yet they would have reached sanctuary in Canada had they known where the boundary was located.

Once again Joseph went east on a visit to New York City as the guest of Buffalo Bill Cody, the showman. He spoke at the commencement exercises at the Carlisle Indian School in Carlisle, Pennsylvania, and then in a final effort in 1893 he went to Washington to petition Theodore Roosevelt to grant his tribe permission to return to the Wallowa Valley. Permission was denied.

White men had taken over the beautiful homeland of the

Nez Percé and they were not going to relinquish it. Their cattle covered the land.

Joseph still loved the valley which contained the bones of his ancestors, but he was never successful in his attempts to go home.

Sitting before his fire on September 21, 1904, he suddenly fell forward and died. The agency physician said grimly, "He died of a broken heart."

It could well have been true. Few men, red or white, ever had more reason for such a demise.

CRAZY HORSE

[1842–1877]

By the time the young Crazy Horse reached the Brûlé village on the Bluewater, a tributary of the Platte, it was nearly dusk. The sky was crisscrossed with jagged streaks of lightning. Off to the west he could hear the rumble of thunder as the storm drew near.

Earlier that day he'd set out from the village where he was visiting his uncle, Spotted Tail, to search for a lost pony. He'd heard no sound of gunfire as he returned, but for some time he had smelled gunsmoke, and now he caught the odor of burning buffalo robes.

A pall of smoke hung over the Brûlé camp, far heavier, and of a darker color, than the smoke of campfires. The other boys with him, frightened, had headed down toward the Sioux Agency on the Platte.

Eyes fixed on the smoke cloud which the thirteen-year-old boy knew could only have come from guns and burning Indian lodges, Crazy Horse hurried toward the camp.

Everyone in the Brûlé village had known that morning that there were white soldiers coming up the Platte to apprehend some young bucks who had held up a stagecoach and some who, the summer before, had killed some white soldiers outside Fort Laramie.

94

These marching bluecoats were coming up the river with wagon guns to avenge the deaths of some white civilians and soldiers, but Crazy Horse, who'd witnessed the killing of the soldiers at Laramie, could not understand this.

The summer before, the white man's year 1854, a detachment of bluecoats had come out from Fort Laramie to the Sioux camp a short distance north of them. A broken-down cow, a stray from a Mormon wagon train moving along the "Holy Road"—so called because no one was supposed to harm anybody traveling along it—had been killed by some young Indian men. The bluecoats had come out of the fort to avenge the killing of the cow. The soldiers had had little else to do at Fort Laramie, that tiny island in a sea of red men, because there had been peace, then, between the red men and the white.

Laughing boisterously, the white soldiers had come, led by an eager young lieutenant, on that hot August day and fired into the Sioux village. They had been killed, themselves, and rightly so, but now more bluecoats had come out to punish the killers. This was wrong!

Besides, who could tell which of the young bucks had fired at the whites down at Laramie, and who would ever tell which Indians had stopped the stagecoach? Still, the bluecoats were coming up the Bluewater from the Platte, but Spotted Tail's people had made no move to run, thinking that they were innocent of any wrongdoing.

Other tribes had gone to the reservations, but this Brûlé village, just back from a buffalo hunt and with fresh meat drying on the racks, had decided to wait. The bluecoats would find no bad Indians in their village.

Crazy Horse, seeing the pall of smoke far to the south, sensed that something terrible had happened. Too often in the past the bluecoats had shot first and asked their questions later. He hurried on through the dusk, the smell of gunsmoke becoming stronger as he approached the village.

Now he reached a little bluff overlooking the village along the creek, and in the gloom, illuminated now and then by flashes of lightning, he saw that the village was no longer there.

Terrible things had happened here. He saw abandoned lodge coverings, lodge poles, piles of burning camp equipment, and then dark shadows on the ground—his people, his relatives.

The storm came closer. Dismounting from his pony Crazy Horse went down the bluff, pausing here and there at the bloodied clumps on the ground, frozen in death, the Brûlés.

He, himself, was an Oglala Sioux. His mother had been a Brûlé and he'd been visiting in the Brûlé camp of his uncle.

Horrified, he paused at each of the lifeless forms scattered on the ground, recognizing some of the people—women, children, boys with whom he'd splashed happily in the creek only the day before.

The trail of the soldiers was easily to be followed. Their iron-shod horses left deep marks in the soft earth. The shoe prints of the walking soldiers led downstream toward the Platte. There were moccasin prints, too, indicating that Brûlés were being taken down to Fort Laramie as prisoners.

Crazy Horse followed the trail for a short distance until he could hear the soldiers up ahead of him moving through the darkness. He could hear them laughing. He didn't know the words because he could not understand the white man's tongue, but the soldiers were singing a song they had just made up:

> We did not make a blunder,
> We rubbed out Little Thunder,
> And we sent him to the other side of Jordan.

Little Thunder had been the chief of this particul
of Brûlé Sioux, a good man, a man at peace with the

Crazy Horse listened to the singing of the white m
thought of those dark forms on the ground, bodies
and smashed by the great bullets from the wagon gu
white man's cannon.

A terrible anger raged through the young Oglala's
It was one thing to shoot an Indian who had a gun, or
a bow and arrow; it was another thing to fire the wagon
at women and children and babies.

Turning back toward the destroyed camp of the Br
Crazy Horse rode through the rain and the thunder, h
bent, following the trail now of the remaining Brûlés.
found a place a few miles beyond where the warriors h
tried to make a stand, concealing themselves in some pitt
caves along the side of a sand bluff, but the great cann
balls had found them out, blowing caves and men to piece
He saw the places where the cannon balls had gouged grea
holes in the bluff, and here were more dead Brûlés.

The trail continued toward the east and the sand hills beyond. Along the trail he found dead bodies, abandoned travois, camp possessions. The soldiers had still been pursuing
them here.

The rain had stopped and the thunder was only an echo
when he found the Cheyenne woman, another camp visitor,
and the dead little boy with a bullet hole through his chest.
The Cheyenne woman had carried the boy all this distance
from camp.

Crazy Horse took her along with him until they reached
the camp of the Brûlés, but there were few of them left.
Many had been killed or captured. Spotted Tail had been
wounded. There were four bullet holes in his body. Little
Thunder had been wounded, too, shot down at the begin-

ning of the fight, but he'd managed to escape.

Those captured had been taken to the white man's stone-house prisons in Laramie, and few Indians ever came out of the stone houses.

Women had lost husbands and children. Crazy Horse could hear the keening of the wives and mothers; he saw the blood running from the cuts they'd made on their arms and legs in their grief.

And it had all started because of a stray cow which had been shot by some Sioux who'd assumed the white men did not want the animal any more. A spindly, broken-down cow, young Crazy Horse thought bitterly, and a reckless, bored young army officer, fresh out of the white man's army college, who had wanted some action.

Remembering those broken forms along the Bluewater, Crazy Horse swore bitter and eternal vengeance against these white men who had come into Indian country and built their Holy Road directly across the Sioux hunting grounds, who'd set up their army posts wherever they wanted to, frightening off the buffalo.

Some day he, Crazy Horse, would ride as a full-grown warrior against the bluecoats. He would never become a reservation Indian, a "loafer-around-the-fort," like so many he'd seen at Fort Laramie. He would fight the bluecoats till all were gone.

Years later, along a stream known as the Little Big Horn, Crazy Horse, war chief of the Oglala Sioux, thought he saw his dream come true.

He was born about the year 1842 on Rapid Creek near the Black Hills, and it had been a time of peace with the whites. But already the wagons were beginning to move up the Platte River, great white-topped wagons, drawn by many

horses or oxen. As a small boy he'd seen the endless lines of these wagons heading toward the setting sun, toward the place where the white men dug the stuff they called gold. This was foolish because they could not eat gold.

Year after year, growing up in his Oglala village under the leadership of Red Cloud, the chief, he'd seen the white men come into the country. Soon they had a fort, and then a trading post. The bluecoats had come to provide protection for the white men who were going west.

It seemed at times, though, as if it were the Indian who needed protection more than the white man! The whites were scaring away the buffalo, taking away Indian food. It was bored white soldiers, more often than not, who fired their guns just to "kill an Indian."

The whites, too, brought in their firewater which made sodden wrecks out of once proud warriors. Crazy Horse, as a child, had seen this, too.

At first the white men had simply wanted permission to cross the Indian hunting grounds, and then they wanted permission to string up their "singing wires" which they called the telegraph. Crazy Horse saw the tall poles and the wires which talked so mysteriously.

Then they laid the shiny steel tracks for the Iron Horse which thundered and roared across the high Plains. The buffalo were afraid of the Iron Horses and they moved far to the north. Hunting became more difficult.

The Cheyennes, the Kiowas, the Sioux had listened to the white men's overtures of peace and had signed treaties with them, treaties which assured the red men that the newcomers had no intention of taking over the land. The barren, empty Plains were of no use, anyway, to these white men. They were simply passing through to the gold fields, to the lush lands of Oregon to the north and west.

It had seemed to young Crazy Horse that all the white men in the world had gone toward the setting sun and surely there were none left in the land from which they had come.

Growing up beside the Holy Road, Crazy Horse had been aware of the fact that he'd been an object of curiosity to many of the white emigrants who pointed at him and stared curiously.

At first he had not known why the emigrants stared. Then, from looking into the white man's mirror, he'd learned that his hair was much lighter in color than the dark black hair of most Sioux. As a matter of fact, it was almost brown, and his skin much lighter so that he could almost pass for a white boy, and the emigrants along the Holy Road had thought that he might be a young white captive.

There was no white blood in him, though. His mother had been a Brûlé woman and his father was Crazy Horse, the medicine man of the Oglalas. The boy had been called "Curly," in the white man's language, by his young friends in the vicinity of Fort Laramie because his hair, strangely enough, was of a different texture and color from that of the other Indians.

He was different from the others not only in looks but in other ways. Unlike the rest of the young bucks he took no part in the dances, the singing, even though he was very successful in raids against the enemy Crows and Snakes.

Despite the fact that at an early age he'd already counted many coups and was looked upon with respect as one of the bravest of the Oglalas, he never stood up to brag of his exploits, always remaining modestly in the background.

Later in life he took his father's name and was known to red man and white alike as Crazy Horse, the Strange One of the Oglalas.

Although he was the son of a peaceful medicine man the

Oglalas made him one of their war chiefs, a Shirt-wearer, and in the wars against the whites which soon broke out there were always swarms of young bucks following at his heels.

During the 1860's, intermittent war was fought between the white men and the Sioux. Treaties had been signed but the whites all too often broke the treaties. Chiefs like Red Cloud and Spotted Tail, both having been to Washington and seen the power of the whites, soon gave up the struggle, but Sitting Bull of the Hunkpapas, some northern Cheyennes, and the Arapahoes, continued to fight. Crazy Horse's Oglalas sided with the Hunkpapas.

There were now two kinds of Indians on the high Plains —the reservation Indians who had signed the peace treaties and accepted the white man's gratuities, and the "wild ones." These were the hostiles who still maintained the old ways, living far north of the Platte, hunting the buffalo.

As a grown man Crazy Horse knew he could never live at peace with the whites. The white men were no longer just moving across the land toward the gold fields. They'd begun to settle in the area, in violation of all the treaties signed by Red Cloud and by Spotted Tail and others.

They were destroying hundreds of thousands of buffalo, at first shooting them for meat for the work crews on the railroads; then later shooting them for the robes or the heavy leather to be used as belting in the great factories to the east, or just for sport.

As a result, because of the tremendous demand for the robes, the hunters had swarmed into the country with their wagons and their Sharps' buffalo guns, shooting down hundreds of the great shaggy animals in one day. In an incredibly short period of time the once immense herds, numbering in the millions, had been drastically reduced. The wild ones were finding it difficult to bring in meat for their children.

The reservation Indians, the "coffee coolers," had no such problems. They were living on the white man's largess, making an abortive attempt to till the ground and plant wheat and corn, not particularly interested in it. The reservation Indians were content to sit in the shadows of their lodges close to the army posts and wait for the gifts, the rations, the whisky.

It was in the year 1865 in the attacks on white outposts near Fort Laramie that Crazy Horse first came to prominence as a war leader. He led the decoys who drew soldiers out of the post and across a small bridge over the Platte where a number of them were killed.

Again the following year in the dead of the winter it was Crazy Horse who led the decoys who drew the army troops out of Fort Phil Kearny and was instrumental in the massacre of Captain William Fetterman and an entire detachment of bluecoats.

His cool bravery and ability to lead men, not just by words but by actions, made him famous through all the Sioux tribes. His war parties attacked railroad survey crews; they harassed expeditions of white troops moving up the Yellowstone through country they'd solemnly given to the Indians in various peace treaties and had promised never to enter.

The whites were no longer talking in terms of permission to cross Indian territories, or even of treaties guaranteeing hunting grounds forever. Too much blood had already been shed.

Now, in the year 1876, it was demanded by the Great White Father in Washington that all Plains Indians move to reservations at once or be considered enemies and hunted down like animals. The wild ones in bands led by Sitting Bull of the Hunkpapas, Crazy Horse of the Oglalas, as well as elements of the Cheyennes under Two Moons, and some Blue Clouds, Arapahoes, refused to come in.

All treaties with the red men had been abrogated. Even the Black Hills which the Plains tribes looked upon as sacred, and where they made their medicine, cut their lodge poles, and spent the hot summer months, had earlier been invaded by an army of gold miners.

In order to bring the wild ones into subjection the War Department was sending three armies north of the Platte River. From the south General George Crook was ordered to proceed with an army of cavalry and infantry. From the west, the Montana gold country, General John Gibbon was marching east with another force of infantry. From the east, Fort Abraham Lincoln on the Missouri, a still larger body of infantry and cavalry was heading west under the over-all command of General Alfred Terry.

The three-pronged movement was intended to squeeze the hostiles in the middle and kill or capture every one of them. Leading the Seventh Cavalry detachment with General Terry's command was the Civil War hero, Colonel George Armstrong Custer. Custer was a dashing cavalry leader who'd fought the tribes south of the Platte. At the time of the march, Colonel Custer was about the same age as Crazy Horse, in the middle thirties.

A great council of the hostiles had been held by Sitting Bull that spring of 1876, a Sun Dance had been conducted, and the federation of tribes was still intact, cognizant of the fact that white soldiers were heading in their direction.

There were probably as many as ten to fifteen thousand Indians, three or four thousand of them warriors, in the great camp which moved constantly up the ladder of rivers flowing into the Yellowstone—the Powder, the Tongue, the Rosebud, and finally the small mountain stream rising in the Big Horn Mountains and emptying into the Big Horn River, the Little Big Horn.

When it was learned that many white soldiers were camped on the Rosebud, Crazy Horse led a band of a thousand fighting men to hit at General Crook's army. He sent the soldiers reeling back in a bitterly fought battle in which the Oglala chief was nearly successful in luring a large detachment of Crook's troopers into a dead-end canyon where all of them would have been slaughtered.

Crazy Horse did blunt this prong of the drive, though, and Crook, with his dead and wounded, was held up for days while Colonel Gibbon and General Terry were forming a juncture on the Yellowstone River, sending out search parties to locate the main Indian village.

The victorious Crazy Horse and his braves returned to the big camp on the Little Big Horn, and it was here, on June 25, 1876, only eight days after the fight against Crook, that George Armstrong Custer, on an advance scout with his Seventh Cavalry, located the Indian camp.

Without further reconnaissance, and without really ascertaining how strong the camp was or how many fighting men it contained, Custer hit it from two different points.

First, he had divided his small command of less than seven hundred men, sending one detachment out to search for Indians. Then another detachment under the command of Major Marcus Reno moved along one bank of the Little Big Horn, while Custer and the larger body of troops advanced on the opposite side of the stream. Behind them came the pack train—no wagons, no cannon. Custer had not wanted them as they slowed him down.

He had a little over two hundred men with him as he

moved along the Little Big Horn with the intention of crossing over and hitting at the village. He had no knowledge
that the Indian village extended for nearly ten miles along
the stream. He had seen only the nearer lodges, and as
they'd been hunting for hostiles for a long, long time, he was
resolved that the Indians would not get away this time.

Major Reno's smaller force charged the camp, which was
on his side of the river, while Custer was still moving his
troops upstream, out of sight behind the bluffs along the opposite bank.

At the first sound of guns, red riders appeared from every
direction, repulsing Reno's charge and then chasing the soldiers back along the stream, across it, and up onto a ridge
where they were besieged.

Crazy Horse, leading his Oglala warriors, was in this fighting along the stream when Custer came down to the river's
edge about two miles away with the main body of the Seventh Cavalry, approximately 215 strong.

Here some Cheyenne warriors attacked him and he was
possibly killed at this point, although this fact has never
been definitely proved. At any rate, his troops retreated up
along the ridges above the stream.

By now almost all the Indians who had chased Major
Reno's column back across the river had turned, galloped
upstream, and were crossing, driving Custer's troops back.

Hundreds, and then thousands, of red riders splashed
across the shallow fording place, eagle-wing whistles shriek-
ing, the watching women and children on the opposite hills
keeping up a high, keening sound.

The warriors drove the confused, hapless detachment of
bluecoats back up the ridges, slaughtering them mercilessly.
Many of the troops tried to fight back, but some, realizing almost immediately that the fight was hopeless and that they

might be taken captive, turned their guns on themselves. The battle could not have lasted more than an hour or so. The last small body of troopers, Custer with them, dead or alive, finally reached a high eminence above the stream where they made a vain but valiant attempt to hold off the swarms of red men.

The Indians were on foot, moving up closer and closer to the besieged bluecoats on the high ridge. Previously, Crazy Horse had led a large body of red riders across the stream and around behind the ridge, cutting off further retreat.

In a matter of minutes the fight was over. The hostiles sent clouds of arrows into this last pocket of resistance; they kept shooting their guns until no more sounds came from the small band of bluecoats crouched behind dead horses.

The red warriors surged forward, swinging hatchets, and the battle of the Little Big Horn was over. Every white man was dead.

The men still on the ridge under Major Reno were eventually saved when General Gibbons' column came to their relief, and the members of the great Indian camp, after setting the grass afire, retreated toward the Big Horn Mountains.

It was the high water mark in the fight against white encroachment. The great Indian federation broke up; its strength was also its weakness.

On the high Plains great bodies of Indians could not exist for any length of time. Forage and game ran out. The small bands had to separate.

Sitting Bull's Hunkpapas moved north. By fall a large white army was on his trail, driving him up toward his ultimate refuge in Canada.

The Cheyennes, hit by another strong white force, surrendered, and the Cheyenne people were put on the reservation.

Only Crazy Horse and small bands of Sioux were still at large. They were driven like so many flocks of sheep by the white forces in the field and they gave up one by one. Finally, only Crazy Horse refused to come in.

His people suffered terribly during the bad winter of 1876–77. In the early part of January, 1877, General Nelson Miles struck his village, but Crazy Horse and his band managed to get away.

All through the summer of 1877 he held out, even though the Sioux were finished. There was no game; the buffalo were gone. White men made all kinds of overtures to bring him in. He was promised his own reservation wherever he wanted it.

Reluctantly, only half-believing these promises, Crazy Horse came in with his Oglalas, and his wife, Black Buffalo Woman, who had contracted the white man's tuberculosis. Previously, his only daughter, a much beloved child, had died of the same sickness.

Relying upon the white man's promises, he surrendered, but there was no special reservation for the Oglalas. There were no special considerations.

The whites were still suspicious of him, knowing him to be the chief Sioux war leader. They expected him momentarily to pull out with his warriors and begin another Indian war.

He was brought into Camp Robinson, the army post adjoining the Oglala Reservation, supposedly for a conference with the post commander, but when the detail of soldiers guarding him led him to the army guardhouse, and he saw the wan, shackled Indian prisoners inside, the barred windows, he made a break for freedom.

An army guard lunged at him with his bayonet and Crazy Horse went down, the bayonet through his body.

"Tell the people," he said mournfully, on his deathbed, "that I can't help them, any more."

He'd done what he could for his people but it had not been enough. At long last the high Plains were empty; the buffalo were gone; the Indians were gone; the plows of the white men were churning up the buffalo grass. It was the end of a way of life for a free people.

SITTING BULL

[1837–1890]

I<small>T WAS LATE</small> Sunday afternoon, June 25, 1876, when Sitting Bull walked his big black horse across the shallow ford of the Little Big Horn River and then on up the grades where the white soldiers had fallen in battle that day.

It had been blisteringly hot, with no breeze stirring. A pall of black gunsmoke still hung over the battlefield where thousands of Sioux, Cheyenne, and Arapaho warriors had defeated the force of several hundred United States troopers who'd hit at the huge Indian village along the stream.

Now the whites were all dead except for the handful of bluecoats still pinned down on the bluff beyond sight of the battlefield.

The black horse moved carefully up the series of ridges which rose from the willows along the Little Big Horn. The horse moved around groups of Indian women, children, and men who were still stripping the bodies of the soldiers, taking their clothing, boots, and equipment, oftentimes mutilating the bodies, as was the Sioux custom, so that when entering the Happy Hunting Grounds the enemy would be minus a trigger finger, an arm, a leg.

The Hunkpapa Sioux chieftain, nearly forty years of age at this time, frowned and shook his head. Several times he advised the people to "leave the dead alone and go back to the village."

The bluecoats who had charged along the river on one side and been repulsed, and these who'd tried to cross the stream farther down, had been very foolish men. White soldiers were often very foolish.

There could not have been more than three hundred bluecoats who had hit at the village, a village which consisted of, perhaps, twelve thousand people.

Watching the battle from across the stream, he had seen how few white soldiers there were in the attack, and how quickly and easily they had been destroyed.

It had not even been a big fight. Hunkpapa warriors, some of them carrying dripping scalps, had ridden across the stream to tell him that the white soldiers had been destroyed.

Sitting Bull had seen the slender, grim-faced, painted, Oglala war chief, Crazy Horse, go by with his usual train of warriors, heading back toward the ridge where the remaining bluecoats were desperately fighting off the red horde gathered around them.

Upstream, he heard the shooting from the besieged troopers on the bluff, and he rode among the dead, the whitened bodies flecked with red, scattered like so many white stones on the rough grass.

A young buck went by wearing a soldier's blue coat, blue forage cap, and blowing discordantly on a captured army bugle. Small boys ran behind him, shouting. One boy clutched a wad of green paper, which the white man called money. He threw the green paper into the air and watched it flutter to the grass. No one picked it up.

The women shouted, also, except the few who'd lost men in battle. Their voices were raised in bitter, keening cries to the brassy sky. Long knives flashed as the new-made widows cut themselves in sign of mourning.

Sitting Bull rode his great black horse over the battlefield and then turned and went back to the village, to his wives, his children. He had not been in this fight; he had a son who'd fought against the bluecoats; his place, as an older man, and a medicine man, too, had been with the women and children, protecting them.

Detractors said later that the Sioux chief, Sitting Bull, had been skulking in his lodge while the fight with George Armstrong Custer's Seventh Cavalry was taking place, but these charges were not true. No Indian had ever accused Sitting Bull of cowardice. His record as a fighting man up to the time of the Little Big Horn fight was impeccable. He'd probably counted more coups against enemy warriors than any of his people with the possible exception of the fierce Crazy Horse.

It was the younger men who'd streaked across the tiny stream to fight the bluecoats; it was the young men who now surrounded the remnants of those foolish white men, a few hundred in number, who'd tried to destroy the greatest Indian village ever assembled on the American continent.

The Hunkpapa war chief and medicine man had been born along Willow Creek in what was later the state of North Dakota about the year 1837. He'd ridden against Crow and Snake enemies from age fourteen on, counting innumerable coups. Because of his bravery in the field there were always many young men who wanted to ride with him when he went out on a horse-stealing raid against the Crows.

Soon, because of his exploits in the field, he was leading war parties and was recognized as a war chief. Later in life, because of his wisdom, and powers of divination, he became a medicine man, also, and probably the best-known Indian west of the Mississippi.

He was a Hunkpapa, largest of several branches of the Sioux Nation—Oglalas, Brûlés, Miniconjous, Santees. Along with the northern Cheyennes and the Arapahoes, the Sioux were engaged in this task of holding back the whites north of the Platte River.

For some time, because the Hunkpapas lived a considerable distance north of the Platte and the line of army forts situated there, and north of the regular wagon trails, Sitting Bull and his Hunkpapas had not been too involved in the fight. There had been brushes with survey crews, with white buffalo-hunting parties, and isolated ranchers, but the Hunkpapas had not suffered at the hands of the whites as had the Brûlés and the Oglalas.

Red Cloud's Oglalas, and Spotted Tail's Brûlés, had been maltreated on more than one occasion by the whites. Red Cloud had been duped into signing treaties; now Red Cloud, once a great fighter, was a reservation Indian, a "coffee cooler."

Because of the continued resistance of the northern, non-reservation tribes—the Hunkpapas, the Miniconjous, Crazy Horse's band of Oglalas—the whites had finally offered peace. They'd stipulated in a peace treaty that "all of the country north of the Platte River, and east of the Big Horn Mountains, was to be Indian Territory" and that "no white person or persons, shall be permitted to settle upon it, or occupy any portion of the same, or, without consent of the Indians, to pass through the same."

Almost before the ink was dry on the treaty document, though, the white men were again on the move. Colonel Custer entered the Black Hills with a survey party. Custer's glowing report sent thousands of miners into the territory, a territory which "no white person or persons shall be permitted to settle upon or occupy without the consent of the Indians."

The gold hunters built towns in the Black Hills. A railroad was being planned far to the north; survey crews were already in the field without the consent of the Indians. It was one of the most brazen abrogations of a treaty in United States history and can be accounted for only by the fact that there were two sets of people operating against the Indians. There were the civilians in Washington, who made the treaties, and then there were the military in the field who on occasions disregarded these same treaties.

In the spring of 1876 Sitting Bull called a great council of the non-reservation bands, and great swarms of Indians gathered near the Black Hills. A Sun Dance was held and plans were made to present a united front to the white man.

The United States Government in the winter of 1875–76 had decreed that all Indians come in to the reservations. Sitting Bull, Crazy Horse, and other non-reservation chiefs disregarded the decree.

Accordingly, in the spring of 1876, the military sent a three-pronged army into the northern Plains. At the Little Big Horn, one prong of the invading force under Custer was blunted, as a second prong led by General Crook had been.

After the Big Horn fight and the massacre of Custer, the great Indian encampment broke up. Crazy Horse and the Oglalas went one way; the Cheyennes and the Arapahoes another. Sitting Bull's Hunkpapas drifted toward the north, with General Nelson "Bearcoat" Miles and a large force of cavalry and infantry after them.

When General Miles' force caught up with the Hunkpapas near the Canadian border, Miles insisted that Sitting Bull and his people give up and enter one of the reservations.

The Hunkpapa chieftain said flatly, "No Indian that ever lived loved a white man, and no white man ever loved an Indian. God Almighty made me an Indian, but not a reservation Indian, and I don't intend to be one."

General Miles' force hit at the retreating Hunkpapas, but Sitting Bull fought them off, still moving toward the north. Through the winter of 1876–77 more and more bluecoats took up the chase after the Hunkpapas, but in February of 1877 Sitting Bull crossed the border and found refuge in Canada, the Grandmother's Country.

The Cheyennes that terrible winter had been apprehended and placed on reservations; Crazy Horse had eventually been forced to come in, and then had been killed by a bluecoat guard. Of all the Sioux who had fought against the whites only Sitting Bull was still alive and free.

The Hunkpapas were now fugitives from their country, permitted to live in Canada only because of the leniency of the Canadian authorities, and here for four years, until 1881, Sitting Bull maintained his independence.

Even in Canada, though, the buffalo were disappearing. Canada, too, was a cold country for a people who were accustomed to wintering much farther to the south. The people became homesick; they wanted to see relatives and friends in the other tribes across the border.

In 1881, Sitting Bull surrendered to the American force at Fort Buford, and the Hunkpapas went to the reservation at Standing Rock, North Dakota.

In the States, Sitting Bull found himself quite a noted figure. He was looked upon as the "Slayer of Custer," and Buffalo Bill Cody, the showman, signed him on with his

Wild West Show and took him East where he learned to sign his name and sell his autograph. He soon grew tired of this, though.

"White men talk too much," the chief said. "To my ears it is like the noise of waters which man can't stop."

He was glad to go back home to the reservation where he was looked upon by his people as their chief and leader.

During the late 1880's, another red Messiah, similar to Tecumseh's brother, the Prophet, had arisen among the Paiutes far to the west, and he was preaching that soon all the whites would be destroyed and the buffalo would be roaming the great Plains as before.

The followers of this Messiah wore white buckskin shirts and danced a special dance called the "Ghost Dance." Medicine shirts, carefully prepared, were supposed to protect the Indians from bullets.

To thousands of Indians on reservations throughout the West the Messiah's message brought new hope. From reservation to reservation the Ghost Dance spread, reaching eventually to the Standing Rock Agency where Sitting Bull was located.

Sitting Bull, a medicine man, himself, had nothing to do with the new Messiah and the Ghost Dancers of the new religion, but white authorities at Standing Rock assumed that if an uprising came he would be the logical man to lead it as he was the most respected chief in the country.

On December 15, 1890, a party of Indian police came to the village of Sitting Bull to apprehend him. According to later newspaper reports, "Sitting Bull resisted arrest and was shot down." He was fifty-three years of age.

Three hundred of his Hunkpapas, under a sub-chief, Big Foot, jumped the reservation, assuming they would be meeting the same fate as Sitting Bull. They were pursued by five hundred cavalrymen, many from the Seventh Cavalry which had fought on the Little Big Horn.

The cavalry force quickly overtook the straggling Hunk-papas in the bitter cold at a place called Wounded Knee Creek.

The Hunkpapas were ordered to surrender. With only a hundred fighting men in the band, and only a few guns, Sitting Bull's people agreed to give up.

Four Hotchkiss machine guns were trained on the Hunk-papas as they sat in the snow, surrounded by nervous troopers. There was no doubt that a few rifles were still concealed under Indian blankets even though most of them had been given up.

Arrangements were being made to bring the recalcitrants back to the reservation when suddenly a shot rang out. No one is positive who fired the shot or why, but the troopers opened up with the machine guns and with rifles.

The desperate Hunkpapas tried to run in every direction but were shot down in the snow, men, women, children, at what has been called the "Battle of Wounded Knee." Big Foot, himself, was killed, and only a handful of survivors were herded back to the reservation.

The remainder lay frozen in the snow, grotesque figures, rigid in death, arms reaching toward the cold Plains' sky. It was as if they were asking for mercy—a mercy they'd never received from the whites who had hounded them from the shores of the Atlantic all the way across a continent.

There was no more Indian resistance anywhere. The Indian became a reservation Indian, a prisoner in his own land. It was the end of a people, a people who had fought for their independence and their own way of life against an invading force. Usually the pattern had been the same—friendly overtures on the part of Indians welcoming white men to the country, Massasoit and his braves bringing in deer to the feast. Then the gradual encroachment by the whites.

Even the Sioux had greeted Lewis and Clark in 1804 with the uplifted hand of friendship. The Ottawas, Shawnees, the Seminoles, the Cherokees, the Apaches, the Kiowas, had permitted white men to enter their country, offering them friendship and aid, but soon the whites in increased numbers had heartlessly taken over their lands.

Resistance by the Indians brought the military to the scene, and in the course of time there were no more Indians. In refutation, the whites put it this way, in the words of William Henry Harrison to the Indiana Legislature:

> Is one of the finest portions of the globe to remain in a state of nature, the haunts of a few wretched savages, when it seems destined by the Creator to give support to a large population, and be a seat of civilization, of science, and true religion?

As far as the white man was concerned, that was the issue, and for better or worse it prevailed.

A LOOK FORWARD

ACCORDING TO most historians, when Christopher Columbus nudged his little ships in toward the sandy shore of San Salvador in the West Indies in the year 1492 there may have been between 15 and 20 million Indians in the Americas. Approximately 850,000 lived within the present boundaries of the United States, with the vast bulk of them below the Rio Grande River.

By the year 1860, of the 850,000 Indians in the United States, 510,000 had been decimated by the constant wars, by epidemics, and by the systematic oppression of the whites. By the year 1910, the total number of Indians in the United States had dropped to 220,000, and the situation was so serious that the term "vanishing American" was not a misnomer.

The red man in America was disappearing from the scene as the buffalo had disappeared from the high Plains.

After 1910, though, better health care and an increasing Indian birth rate nearly tripled the red population. It is estimated now that there are over 700,000 red men within the confines of the United States, with 450,000 still living on some 284 reservations. The reservations range from the one-acre Strawberry Valley *rancheria* in Yuba County, California, to the enormous Navaho Reservation, the size of the state of West Virginia, in Arizona, New Mexico, and Utah.

Various American Presidents and administrations have sought ways to accommodate the tribes, and in the beginning always with the thought in mind of assimilation. President James Monroe, as far back as 1807, wrote, "The hunter or savage state requires a greater extent of territory to sustain it than is compatible with the progress and just claims of civilized life, and must yield to it."

As has been seen, Andrew Jackson and William Henry Harrison held similar views. The red man had to be assimilated into the American culture one way or the other. Extermination was not mentioned, of course, but the policies of the federal government, the acts of politicians and land-hungry manipulators, came close to accomplishing this.

In the days of Supreme Court Justice John Marshall, at the very beginnings of our nation, the Court stipulated that the Indian tribes were "dis-nations," with which the United States had to deal legally by treaties.

The treaties were many between the white men and the red, and the end results were always the same. Treaties solemnly signed by white officials were not honored.

After the final slaughter at Wounded Knee the task of assimilation was begun seriously. Tribes were all on reservations, policed by the army and administered by the Department of the Interior. Avaricious Indian agents, and profiteers working on the fringes of the reservations, continued the steady, grinding process of destroying the red men.

On the reservations, the Indians were out of sight, and, hopefully, out of mind. They were supposed to till the soil, learn the white man's ways, and gradually, over the course of years, become white in every respect.

There was a fly in the ointment, however. The red men

generally refused to become white men.

The Indians had seen enough of the white man's culture not to want it for themselves. Some made the change. The rest simply lived on the reservations, the wards of the government, forbidden to leave, given no opportunities whatever to manage their own affairs, treated as prisoners of war, or, worse, as children.

It was an unhappy and unhealthy situation. The few officials who looked into the matter realized that some adjustments had to be made.

In the year 1887 Congress passed the Dawes General Allotment Act, a law intended to hasten assimilation. The reservations were to be surrendered and divided into family-size farms with each adult Indian to receive 160 acres, and each minor child 80 acres of land. The Indians would receive outright ownership of the land after twenty-five years.

The remaining reservation acreage was to be declared surplus and offered for sale to the whites. Naturally, there were many whites on the fringes of the reservations anxious and willing to pick up Indian lands open to the public.

The plan didn't work. Indians who had been nomadic hunters all of their lives just could not become farmers overnight. Added to this was the fact that many of the reservation lands were not fit for cultivation. White ranchers and farmers had naturally taken over the best lands long before the reservations were established.

There were few real attempts to teach the Indian how to make this transition from hunter to farmer. The Indian male had always been first a warrior and secondly a hunter. Any digging of the soil generally had been done by the women.

Little financial help was given to them, and as a result Indians who did accept the Allotment Act Plan soon leased or sold their properties outright to the whites. By the year 1932 it was estimated that out of 138 million acres of land held by Indians, 90 million had passed over to white ownership.

Many of the Southwestern tribes had resisted the Act entirely, and it was not put into practice in many other territories. Indian males, neither hunters nor farmers, became nonentities, almost non-people. Alcoholism was rampant on reservations which were marked by poverty, squalor, and disease.

The Dawes Act, designed to aid the red man in being assimilated into the white man's culture, had not worked. Part of it was due again to the avarice, the greed, and the indifference of many who were supposed to be assisting these downtrodden peoples.

The Indian was not even a citizen of the United States until the year 1924, when, out of gratitude for services performed by American Indians in World War I, the Snyder Act was passed which conferred citizenship on all Indians. It is wondered who these patriots in World War I were who fought and died for a nation which did not even recognize them as part of its political system.

But making the Indian a citizen of the United States did not even begin to solve his problem. He was still a ward of the government, being supported more or less by Federal monies.

During the Administration of Franklin D. Roosevelt, in the year 1934, the Wheeler-Howard Act, known as the Indian Reorganization Act, sought to change the general policy toward all Indians.

It encouraged self-government by the tribes; it extended financial credit to Indians; and major efforts were made to improve educational and medical facilities. It tried to promote a revival of Indian culture.

Assimilation hadn't worked; it was resolved now that if the red man could not become a white man, at least he could be made a human being, and, perhaps, assimilated on his own terms.

Under the Indian Reorganization Act the tribes on the reservations were permitted to organize their own institutions and to some extent manage their own affairs—always, of course, under the general supervision of the Department of the Interior, and the Bureau of Indian Affairs.

However, a step had been taken in the right direction for the first time since Wounded Knee. Red men were permitted to think for themselves and do for themselves, but with the federal government still footing the bills.

After World War II, however, there were many who began to wonder how long the government would have to pay for the many services to the Indian. It was hoped that sooner or later the government would be able to terminate its relations with the tribes altogether.

Indian self-sufficiency, however, was far from being achieved. The Reorganization Act had not solved all of the Indian problems by any means. Many Indian Bureau officials, agents, field supervisors, had not encouraged their wards to take advantage of the benefits of the new act, and the bureaucrats continued their direction and control of Indian affairs.

Attempts were made by the Indian Bureau to improve the Indian's economic status by relocation programs. Indians were sent off the reservations to different cities, given jobs and homes, and occasionally these efforts were successful. Many more of the relocated Indians failed miserably. Losing their jobs or their homes in resultant periods of depression, they became dislocated persons, ending up on skid row or as welfare applicants.

The "termination" Indian policy failed miserably, also, in the State of Wisconsin where the Menominie tribe, with large lumber holdings on the reservation, had pressure put on them by state politicians to become a self-supporting county, like any other county in the state. The white men reasoned that if the Menominies were making money on their lumber they should support themselves like any other county.

When the reservation did become a county in the state of Wisconsin, the Menominies found themselves paying very high taxes to support the police, hospital, and other services all counties had to provide for their people.

Their savings dwindled; they were threatened with the loss of their homes; there was much mismanagement. Wisconsin found itself saddled with a huge welfare problem, so bad that it had to appeal to the federal government for assistance.

Under President John F. Kennedy this "termination" policy was all but abandoned. New programs were instituted; new educational and vocational training facilities were provided; economic assistance was guaranteed. The United States Public Health Service took over the responsibility for providing medical care to Indians.

Under the "Great Society" programs instituted by President Lyndon Johnson, funds became available for housing, for educational and health programs. Capital and credit were provided to help the tribes gradually become self-supporting. Reservation poverty programs, presented by the Indians, themselves, were to be funded by the federal government.

Now, too, the red men were organizing in such groups as the National Congress of American Indians, and the National Indian Youth Council, putting pressure on the federal government to give them more and more responsibility in the management of their own affairs.

The Indian Commissioner for the Bureau of Indian Affairs met with Indians to formulate policies. On every hand there were now government officials sitting down with Indian representatives from the various tribes and discussing means and methods of improving the condition of the red men.

There was a shift from direct assimilation to what was considered a more gradual acceptance of Indians as Indians. Courses were being taught in schools on Indian culture and history; Indians were involved in the administration of their schools; and the role of the Indian Bureau in Indian affairs was relegated to the position of advisor.

The Indians, from the beginning, had insisted upon maintaining their own culture; they did not want to forget that they were Indians. Young people on the reservations were encouraged to maintain both red and white cultures.

Even so, conditions are still very harsh on almost all reservations throughout the land. The rapid increase in Indian population and the lack of work on or near the reservations have kept the Indians far down the economic scale.

In 1967 statistics showed that the average income of an Indian family in the United States was $1500 per year. Unemployment was as high as 40 and 50 per cent, sometimes as much as 80 per cent on some reservations during the winter season, an incredible figure. At least 90 per cent of Indian housing was unacceptable by any American standards; the dropout rate in the schools was 50 per cent compared to the national average of 29 per cent. Sixty per cent of the American Indians have less than an eighth-grade education.

There has been some improvement in recent years, but the red man is still below other racial groups in matters of earning power, housing, and health.

In July of 1970, President Richard M. Nixon stated that the story of the Indian in America had been marked with "the white man's frequent aggression, broken agreements, intermittent remorse, and prolonged failure. The time has come," he said in his message to Congress, "to break decisively with the past and to create conditions for a new era in which the Indian future is determined by Indian actions and Indian decisions."

The Commissioner of Indian Affairs, Louis R. Bruce, an Indian himself, instituted many reforms in his department, bringing in a number of young, educated Indians as field administrators.

In response to the President's request for a "new and coherent strategy" for Indian self-determination, Commissioner Bruce worked to establish Indian economic systems through the 40-million-dollar employment assistance program. The tribes also were encouraged to make economic-development plans of their own. Such systems are already in operation. Some tribes sell their products by mail order, and various missions, supported by contributions from hundreds of thousands of private citizens all over the land, are aiding the Indians to set up their own cooperatives and businesses.

In another effort to make amends for so many heartless actions in the past, the federal government in 1946 established a special Indian Claims Commission which was to hear and decide upon all Indian claims of unjust land dealings and to award payments for restitution of lands illegally taken.

Naturally, a great many claims were presented by the various tribes—580 as a matter of fact, even one from the Seminoles, the comparative handful still remaining in Florida. The Seminoles claimed payment for the entire State of Florida, maintaining that the land had been worth 40 million dollars at the time it was taken from them after the forcible removal of the tribes to Oklahoma in 1835.

The Seminoles ultimately were awarded 12.3 million dollars in May of 1970, a claim they are still disputing in the courts.

Other claims are being dealt with regularly, the government having paid out over 100 million dollars by 1964. At the present time some 290 Indian claims are still in litigation as the Commission struggles to go through its backlog of claims with its tenure set to expire in April of 1972 unless it is extended.

Bills to implement President Nixon's self-determination doctrine are pending before Congress, which has already voted to restore the sacred Blue Lake to the Taos Pueblo Indians.

The white man is at present attempting to do much to alleviate the conditions under which his red brother lives. The government and its people are finally awakening to the fact that the Indians of the United States have been too long subjected to the suppression of their rights as human beings, and are striving to realize the wish of Chief Joseph that all should be alike—"brothers of one father and one mother, with one sky above us and one country around us, and one government for all."

INDEX